Journey Toward Joy

Life As It Ought To Be

Dennis M. Cahill

Lowbar Publishing Company
Nashville, Tennessee

Published by:
Lowbar Publishing Company
905 S. Douglas Ave.
Nashville, Tennessee 37204
615-972-2842
Lowbarpublishingcompany@gmail.com
www.Lowbarbookstore.com

Author: Dennis M. Cahill
Editor: Ronald L. Kohl
Book Cover Design: Monica Sims
Format Design: Rasel King

Unless otherwise noted, Scripture quotations are from The Holy Bible, English Standard Version, copyright @2001 by Crossway Bibles, a division of Good News Publishers.

Printed in the United States of America
ISBN: 979-8-9904802-0-9

Life As It Ought to Be

the awakening of the people for the awakening of the peoples

ongoing spiritual awakening

wholeness in a broken world

living this day for that day

good news in a bad news world

ordinary people living extraordinary lives

living the gospel way

the people of God living in the power of God

living as a new creation in an old creation world

living the "already" in a world of "not yet"

living by the Spirit in the age of the Spirit

being filled with all the fullness of God

stepping into the supernatural of God

Contents

Endorsements

As Christians, we know that true joy is found in God alone. Yet if we're honest, as Dennis has the courage to be, this head knowledge doesn't always translate into heart experience. If you've ever wondered, "Lord, where are the streams of living water that are to come from my heart?" you will be blessed by this authentic account of one man's breakthrough journey into joy. It offers true and intensely practical insight into the Biblical path to a deep and abiding life of joy in Jesus.

Daniel Henderson, President of Strategic Renewal and Global Director, The 6:4 Fellowship

Dennis Cahill was my pastor for 25 years. He was devoted to the church God had entrusted to him and was a hard-working example that we were happy to follow. But the last years of his ministry among us were different. He was still the same Dennis: sincere, attentive, ready to give aid and comfort and encouragement whenever he could. But there was more to him. More laughter. More peace. More hope. More goodness. Frankly, more gospel. Instead of trying harder to do better, Dennis started saying "more and more" about living life through the power of the gospel. We jokingly called this "Dennis 2.0" because he was so transformed. His new book, *Journey Toward Joy: Life as It Ought to Be,* captures his life-transforming experience and his ongoing practice to help believers live the abundant life that comes from a personal encounter with the joy of the Lord. This book is his story, and I can tell you it is real. I pray that it helps you on your "journey toward joy."

Kathryn Jerabek Davis, Member of Christ Community Church. Piscataway, NJ, and co-creator of the *Sword of the Spirit Devotional Journey*

Journey Toward Joy: Life As It Ought To Be by Dr. Dennis Cahill is a blueprint for soul-searching disciples of Jesus who long to make the mystical union of fellowship in Christ a daily reality. I especially appreciate not only the personal vulnerability but also the practical insights for "ritualizing the joy of the Lord." Having walked closely with Dennis in recent years, I have watched, learned, and benefitted from his deepened spiritual journey, and his life and presence has strengthened our congregation's experience of intimacy with God.

Dr. Michael Hearon, Lead Pastor, First Presbyterian Church, Augusta, GA

Journey Toward Joy: Life As It Ought to Be is the story of how God can change our lives no matter when and no matter who we are. It is also a guide on how to pursue that change with helpful illustrations and very practical application. Thank you, Dennis, for our many years of friendship and for the privilege of seeing this take place in your life. And thank you for sharing this honest and hope-inspiring story!

Rick Ravis, Co-pastor with the author at Christ Community Church for 30 years

Dennis and I have been coworkers within the Bible Fellowship Church denomination for many years. As members of the BFC Executive Board, Dennis and I would travel together to visit and serve with a couple of our smaller, struggling churches. Each trip would encompass at least two hours of uninterrupted conversation, during which Dennis would share with me what he was learning and how it was transforming his life. His story was broken up into the pieces he was experiencing that week and how he could see God working all things out for God's good (and our ultimate benefit), according to God's purposes (which we didn't often know). Every trip ended with Dennis praying for the church we had just visited, and for me personally—which was always needed and welcomed. This book is the compilation of the transformation that occurred in Dennis' life, and I can attest that it is all true! Reading it should, must, and will challenge your heart into living *life as it ought to be*.

Dr. David T. Allen, Executive Director of the Bible Fellowship Church

All great personal and corporate revivals have included a spiritual awakening, and so it was for Dennis Cahill. Dennis has shown us that ministry can be performed without the power of the Spirit, which many of us have experienced in our own ministry. And yet, he has opened to us a window into his soul (heart) and allowed us to witness his journey from a dry parched land to one flowing with milk and honey. This was no mere academic exercise for Dennis, it was truly a spiritual awakening. We are invited down a similar path should we choose. This little book, *Journey Toward Joy*, is a roadmap for you and me on our way to *life as it ought to be*.

Dr. Mike Phillips, Associate Pastor, First Presbyterian Church, Augusta, GA

Dedication

I dedicate this book to the one person, more than anyone else, who has walked with me through life: my wife Patricia. In the years I struggled, she never gave up on me and always encouraged me. She is my joy.

Acknowledgments

The experiences I speak about in this book were lived out in the church I served for 35 years, Christ Community Church in Piscataway, NJ. It was in that community of faith that I learned to live the gospel. The people and leaders of Christ Community Church walked with me in my struggles, never gave up on me, and encouraged me as I took steps on the gospel path. I will be grateful for all eternity!

Other than my wife Patricia, Pastor Rick Ravis, my co-pastor at Christ Community, is the person with whom I have lived life most closely over the last three decades. Every Monday morning (except for the pandemic years, when we met online), we would meet in my study to ponder the Sunday just past, to pray, and to plan for the coming week. Rick saw with greater clarity than most my inadequacies but never stopped encouraging me in the gospel. He is one person I can always count on to encourage me when my ideas are good and to push back when they are not so good. That is, I believe, the essence of a friend.

Dick Vroman is a seminary friend who moved to north-central New Jersey to help in the adventure of beginning a new church. He has been the faithful Director of the Children's Ministry at Christ Community Church for over three decades. He consistently called me back to the Scriptures in all our decisions. He is a friend for time and eternity.

My brother Gere has been a primary reading partner in the writing of this book. His insightful comments created a lot more work for me (and made for a much better book)! Thanks, Gere!

My friend and fellow pastor, Ron Kohl, spent hours editing this manuscript and gave many insightful comments.

My son Jonathan read the manuscript in its many stages, offered many comments, and was a primary think-out-loud partner. His Ph.D. dissertation[1] on the role of emotion in the Christian experience helped me put words to my experience.

My daughters Megan and Sarah have helped me to learn what it means to live out my ideas in real-life relationships. Both have pushed back on the agendas I too often bring into relationships. They have helped me to understand that the gospel is not first about doing; it is first about being.

My niece Christa has helped me understand how to apply this book to the real afflictions of life.

Many others have read and given encouragement—too many to list. Thanks to all of you!

---

[1] Jonathan's dissertation has been rewritten and printed in book form: Jonathan M Cahill, *Emotions, Moral Formation, and Christian Politics: Rereading Karl Barth* (New York: T&T Clark, 2024).

Foreword

I'm an older guy. I've been around the block in my business career and life and have been exposed to thousands of people. I know how hard it is for us humans to change our personalities as we grow older. Generally, we don't change who we are as people all that much as we age.

That's why I suggested to my brother Dennis that he consider writing a book about the dramatic changes that took place in his life—all of a sudden—when he was over 60 years of age. Never have I been exposed to someone who changed so dramatically, and virtually overnight. I didn't think that anyone could change that much in such a positive fashion at that age. Anyway, it seemed to me to be something the rest of us might want to know about, so I suggested that he consider writing a book about the reason for the change in his life.

All of his life, Denny was quiet, introspective, and reserved. "Outgoing" and "humorous" were not words you would have used to describe Denny. Not a touchy-feely sort of person. A very good person but one who kind of kept things to himself. Smart. I always thought of Denny as likely destined for academia and would never have expected him to become a pastor of a church—a career that is much more touchy-feely. And he went through a very difficult period in his life when the responsibilities of being a pastor seemed to be more than he could bear. He was so full of anxiety and fear of being inadequate for the role.

Then, suddenly, I noticed that I had a new brother—a person who seemed so happy and full of purpose and direction, someone who had become so outgoing that he now consistently walks up to complete strangers and strikes up a conversation on almost any topic. A person who now tells jokes (okay, his jokes aren't always good, but he does have a sense of humor now!). He's still not touchy-feely, but I think that kind of runs in our family. How the heck did all of this happen? Man, what a change. That was several years ago, and the "new" Denny still remains with us.

Anyway, I'd never seen anything like it: a change that dramatic and for the good! So, I asked him if he could explain what brought about this dramatic change in his life to the rest of us—who wouldn't want to experience the kind of change that Denny has? And that's what caused this book. Now for the hard part: Can the rest of us figure out how to experience a change like Denny's? I think that's Denny's hope: that his story will help the rest of us to experience a change similar to what he did.

Gerry Cahill, Brother of the author and former President and CEO of Carnival Cruise Lines

Preface

≈

How did this short book come about? In 2019, Clara cut my hair. While she snipped away, Clara and I always had interesting conversations, often about spiritual things and sometimes about my sermons. One day, as I was leaving the salon, I said to Clara, "If I gave you a book to read, would you read it?" She told me she wasn't a big reader, but she would give it a try. I wrote "Book for Clara" in my to-do app and scheduled the reminder to come up before my next haircut.

The week before my next hair-cutting appointment, the reminder popped up: "Book for Clara." I searched my bookshelves for just the right book for her, but nothing seemed quite right. I asked my co-pastor, Rick Ravis, for suggestions. He made a few. I went online searching…but nothing seemed like the right fit.

At 6 a.m. on the morning of my 9:30 a.m. hair appointment, I realized I had no book and that I would have to tell Clara, "Sorry, no book." But then the thought came to me: "You write it." I replied, "Lord, you do realize that my appointment is in three hours, don't you?"

I went into my study and rather quickly typed out a 4–5-page introduction. That didn't prove difficult because, for two years, I had been pondering and living out the events and ideas recorded in this book. I took the introduction to Clara and said, "I wrote this for you…and each time I come to get my hair cut, I will bring another chapter!" I think she was touched—she gave me a hug!

So, this book was written for Clara, but not just for Clara. It is for all people who desire a more intimate, authentic experience of God—for *life as it ought to be*. Maybe it was written for you.

PART ONE

Spiritual Awakening

~≈~

Would you join me on an adventure into the unknown?

Recently, I heard this definition of the word "adventure": *an adventure is a journey with an unknown outcome.* I would add to that definition—though the outcome is unknown to us, it is always known to God. This book is an invitation into the unknown. Neither you nor I know the specifics of what God will do in your life as you begin this journey. We can only know that he tells us that we are stepping into the life that he intends for us.

I was a joyless, powerless, struggling pastor who, late in life and ministry, caught a glimpse of God's glory. On a winter day in 2017, he opened my eyes to his beauty and wonder. I came face to face with my own inadequacy and sin. Then, I experienced something new—the joy and power of Jesus. I discovered in my uncertainty the certainty of God's empowering presence. I will never be the same.

I invite you, in the next pages, to join me in this supernatural adventure. I invite you to experience what I call *life as it ought to be.*

CHAPTER ONE

Awakening

~~~

> *"Whether he is a sinner I do not know. One thing I do know, though I was blind, now I see." John 9:25*

"I wish I had no emotions!" I said to myself—and not too long ago! For about nine years I struggled with anxiety and panic attacks and the depression that often accompanies them. As a Christian minister, I made my living talking before the public. But for almost a decade, every Sunday when I stood before my congregation to speak, I experienced panic, maybe not always a full-blown panic attack, but always a sense of panic. For a time, I experienced what might be called clinical depression. So, it's no wonder I said, "I wish I had no emotions," for all my emotions seemed bad.

Anxiety and panic attacks weren't the only issues because even before that time, I experienced little joy. I was taken captive by the joylessness of my never-ending attempts to please other people. I was driven to be a success for all the wrong reasons. Much too often, I felt like I was playing a role. There isn't much joy in that.

I felt a tension between the life the Bible describes and the life I was living. The Bible tells us we are to "rejoice with joy that is inexpressible and filled with glory" (1 Peter 1:8), that we are to live "to the full" (John 10:10 NIV), and that we are to live with peace "which surpasses all understanding" (Philippians 4:7). None of that was my experience.

This book is the story of my struggle with brokenness and my experience of the supernaturalness of the gospel. This is my story of discovering *life as it ought to be.*

February 2017...

I grew up as an introvert; anyone who knew me would have described me that way. My life was often marked by a paralyzing self-consciousness. People described me as "quiet." Social situations tended to be very difficult. I tried to live in a way that I thought others would find acceptable and would unconsciously compare myself with others. I experienced periodic episodes of depression.

I sought to compensate for my personality inadequacies by reading books, taking graduate courses, and attending conferences. Though most of those things were helpful, none rescued me from the chains of my inward focus and joylessness.

Despite my struggles I did experience a certain level of success. With my wife Patricia and our two children in tow, I moved to Edison, New Jersey in 1986 to be part of a new *Bible Fellowship Church.*[2] When the small core group with which we began dissolved after about 18 months, we restarted in 1989, and this time the church took root and began to grow. Two friends from seminary, Dick Vroman and Rick Ravis, moved to New Jersey with their families in order to be part of this new church, and it continued to grow. After initially renting an elementary school in the town of Edison on Sundays, we progressed to renting a student center on

---

[2] *The Bible Fellowship Church* is the denomination with which I have served for the last three-plus decades. For more information, see www.bfc.org.

the campus of Rutgers University in adjacent Piscataway. By the early 2000s, we sometimes had a Sunday morning attendance of over 300 — many of them college students. I thought I was on the way to ministerial success...but I was still in chains to my fear of people and enslaved to my desire for their approval.

My seeming success was interrupted in 2002. One of my seminary preaching teachers taught us to preach without using any notes to guide us in our speaking. Preaching without notes can be challenging (there's always the fear of forgetting what you want to say), but when done well, there is great freedom in it. I preached note-free for more than a year in the 1990s, but then I went back to using notes, probably because it was easier. In my mind, however, I felt that preaching without notes was better, so on a Sunday in August 2002, I attempted to return to preaching without the use of notes. I had prepared well and stood before the congregation, just me and my Bible. But during the sermon, I struggled with an unexpected and strange feeling, and it was very difficult to finish the sermon. Afterward, I described what had happened to my wife, and she replied, "That sounds like a panic attack." I didn't want that to happen again, so I met with a counselor that week.

But it did happen again — again and again and again. For almost 10 years, I experienced a sense of panic every time I spoke. The panic attacks were accompanied by a more generalized anxiety. One Monday morning, I found myself seated in my office, head in my arms, unable to function. Our church secretary could tell something was wrong, just not what. And then I began to experience what is sometimes called the "fear of fear." I would become extremely nervous in the hours before I was to preach, wondering "Is this the week when I totally fail?"

That led to depression as I wrestled with fears that threatened to overwhelm me. If I can't preach, I can't do my job, and if I can't do my job, I could lose everything. I would lose everything. Who wants a preacher who can't preach?

There were other complications, too. As I wrestled with anxiety, our church went through what I have called "the great decline." For over a decade, we had grown every year; now, we began to lose people each year. Good people, faithful people — people we loved and cared for — left the church. Our attendance figures and finances both trended in a bad direction. Over about eight years, for various reasons, we lost close to half our people. This was not the success I was seeking, the success I had imagined.

While my panic attacks gradually lessened and eventually disappeared by around 2011, the church continued to decline in attendance and finances. Our church leaders realized that if something didn't change, we weren't going to make it. We became desperate — so desperate that we began to pray for the renewing work of the Holy Spirit! My co-pastor Rick and I preached on renewal. Twice, we held what we called "Renewal Conferences." Once we took the whole church away for a weekend renewal retreat at the nearby Pinebrook Retreat Center. Some of us began to meet for prayer on a weekly basis at 5:30 a.m., asking God to give us spiritual renewal.

In the fall of 2016, Rick took an online course on prayer led by Pastor Daniel Henderson: a course on how to lead a church to become a praying church. After completing the course, he recommended that our church leadership read one of Henderson's books, *Old Paths, New Power.*[3] In it, Henderson teaches us to walk the "old paths" of the Word of God and prayer as the primary work of ministry. As I read it, I came to a sad conclusion: I realized that I was a pastor who didn't pray, at least not as I should have. I wanted to pray, I planned to pray, and I tried to pray, but I was busy, life was pressing, and there were sermons to write and emails to answer.

I decided that what I would do is pray for an hour each day. That first morning, I began, as Henderson taught, by seeking God out of the Bible.[4] As I began to praise the Lord in prayer and seek him from a particular passage of the Bible, I was awakened to a fresh vision of the wonder and majesty of God! I began to see with new eyes the beauty of Jesus. My words of praise were not just words but the overflow of my heart. I felt awe and a new sense of God's presence. As I prayed, I forgot my problems and struggles and became caught up in that moment with God himself. And then as I prayed, the light of God's glory began to reveal the depth of my pride, my failure to love God wholly, and the idolatry of my heart.[5] I had long recognized that I was a sinner, but often in a rather abstract way: "We have all sinned." But now I began to understand my pride and rebellion in very specific ways. I confessed my sin, pride, and rebellion as best I could and stepped into the gospel truth of forgiveness. I embraced the gospel as my only hope.

Then, I became aware of an unfamiliar feeling. "What is that?" I wondered. "Oh, that must be joy!" And it was. After all those years

---

[3] Daniel Henderson, Old Paths New Power: *Awakening Your Church Through Prayer and the Ministry of the Word* (Chicago: Moody Publishers, 2016).

[4] Henderson calls his approach to prayer "Scripture-fed, Spirit-led, worship-based prayer." Henderson, *Old Paths*, 125.

[5] Heart idolatry is anything that we hold in our hearts as more important than God himself.

of broken emotions, there was a new song in my heart, a smile on my face, a lilt in my steps. In February 2017, at the age of 63, I experienced spiritual awakening.

CHAPTER TWO

Transformed

❧

…be transformed by the renewal of your mind… Romans 12:2

Transformation

What happened to me was more than an emotional experience that lasted for hours, days, weeks, or even months. It has been transformative. My older brother Gere was one of the first to notice a change in me. On July 4, 2017—less than five months later—Gere sent me this text: "Remind me to tell you something the next time we talk. I've noticed an amazing change in you in the last year." I have always looked up to my brother. He knows me like few others and walked with me through my most difficult days. The day Gere texted me, he had not seen me since the previous summer. We talked on the phone about once a week, but I had never said anything to him about a spiritual experience. Our phone conversations typically focused on the weather, kids, grandkids, and work—my work, his retirement. But when we talked a short time after he'd texted me, Gere said the first thing he'd noticed was that I had developed a sense of humor! And he was right; I had begun to laugh.

From Quiet to Much Less Quiet

As I've mentioned, I was always a bit quiet. No one would ever have called me outgoing. But sometime after that day in February, as I was out riding bikes with my friend and neighbor Satish, he said to me, "You would do well in India!" I responded, "Because...?" "Because you are a people person!" He came to that conclusion having observed that, as we rode, I would often greet passersby and talk with them. I laughed at Satish's comment. That was the first time, in over six decades of life, that anybody had ever called *me* a people person!

Relationships

Relationships were never my strength. I thought that was just the way I was: shy, introverted, not good with small talk, a bit superficial. Fortunately, I had Pastor Rick and my wife Patricia by my side. With their help, somehow, I struggled through in a career that is very relationship-oriented.

Every year, I attended the Bible Fellowship Church's annual leadership conference. Even though I served on committees and boards and spoke several times at the conference, I was always uncomfortable with the relational aspect of the conference. Being self-conscious and a bit awkward in interpersonal conversation for three days is tiring. At the conference's end, I would breathe a sigh of relief. "At least that's over for another year," I thought.

But now, late in life, I am learning how to live in relationship. I am almost tempted to say that relationship is becoming a strength (though those closest to me might remind me that I still have a ways to go). Before 2017, I had acquaintances, colleagues, co-workers, and fellow church members. But now I have friends. I am so grateful! I am learning what it means to develop deep relationships. I am learning to be a friend and to care deeply about others.

A New Power for Preaching

Preaching has been my primary work for the past four decades. Preaching is demanding, exhilarating, and anxiety-producing. At the beginning of 2017 I knew a lot about preaching. I had been preaching for over three decades. I had read many books on preaching. I had completed a doctoral program in preaching with Haddon Robinson, a well-known teacher of preaching. I once helped teach a course in preaching with Dr. Robinson. I even wrote a book about preaching![6] But while others sometimes said I was a good preacher; I had a love/hate relationship with preaching. I loved it when I preached well, and people told me that I had preached well, but the process of preparing and always wondering what people thought was stress-filled. On Sundays when I didn't think I preached well—which was often—I often fell into a pit of self-pity and despair.

Spiritual awakening changed my preaching. It wasn't a matter of technique or sermon structure; I already knew plenty about technique and structure. It was a matter of the heart. When I stopped being obsessed with what people thought of me, when I began to seek the glory of the Father, and when I began to learn what it meant to live by the power of the Spirit, I experienced a new passion and a new confidence as I spoke the words of God. I began to experience what the apostle Paul speaks of as preaching that is a "demonstration of the Spirit and power" (2 Corinthians 2:4).

One Sunday morning, sometime after my experience of renewal, my youngest daughter, Sarah, came home from Rhode

---

[6] Dennis M. Cahill, *The Shape of Preaching: Theory and Practice in Sermon Design* (Grand Rapids: Baker Books, 2007).

Island for a visit. Sarah grew up listening to me speak. After the service that day, Sarah asked my wife, "Do people notice a difference in Dad's preaching?" The answer to Sarah's question was, "Yes, people have noticed." The people of my church saw a new earnestness, love, and power that came not from me but from God at work in me.

A New Ability to Lead

I am an unlikely leader. The results of a leadership assessment I took in 2007 said, "The Profile indicated that you are not a leader; you do not have a leadership aptitude..." This was not good news for someone who made his living in a leadership role! I lacked confidence and was too concerned about what people thought. I wanted to be a good leader; the many leadership books on my bookshelves attested to my desire, but I just wasn't.

My awakening to the power of the gospel also awakened a leadership capability I didn't know I had. At the 2021 Bible Fellowship Church Conference, in which I had two relatively small speaking parts, one of the pastors at the conference whispered in my ear as he walked by, "You are a good leader." He may even be right—but if so, any leadership abilities I may possess are a product of the transforming work of the gospel in me.

It is now 2023. I am two years into "retirement." I have no official leadership role in my church except as an occasional Sunday School teacher. Yet I would not be surprised to learn in eternity that I am having more leadership impact now than I ever did over the decades when I was a main leader in my church in New Jersey.

My True Self

In recent years, I have more and more become my true self: myself as I am in Christ. Frederica Mathewes-Green puts it this way, "The indwelling Christ enables each person to be more himself than he was ever able to be before."[7] The apostle Paul tells us in Ephesians 4:22-24, *"Put off your old self,* which belongs to your former manner of life… and *put on the new self,* created after the likeness of God…"* (emphasis added). The new self is not a different self but the self as it ought to be in Christ.

I met Gary Brill at a ministry fair at Rutgers University in 2019. I was representing Christ Community Church, and Gary was there on behalf of the Humanist Society at Rutgers. We decided to get together for lunch and have met together, as friends, ever since. Now that I have moved to South Carolina, we meet over the Internet. Gary and I are very different. He sees things through the lens of psychology (he is a retired psychology professor) and his agnostic worldview. I see life through the lens of Christian theology and my gospel worldview.

Yet, there is much that we have in common. We discovered that we were born in the same year, the same month, and even on the same day! Both Gary and I care about the big questions of life. *Is there a God? Is there ultimate meaning in life? What happens when we die?* Our conversations are always interesting. I love Gary.

One day at lunch, Gary gave me what I consider the best compliment I've ever received when he said, "I consider you a genuine Christian." I have no greater aspiration than to be a

---

[7] Quoted by Kelly M. Kapic in *You're Only Human: How Your Limits Reflect God's Design and Why That's Good News* (Grand Rapids: Brazos Press, 2022), 17.

genuine follower of Jesus. What Gary saw in me was not "me" playing a role, trying to win the approval of others; he saw the "me" who was beginning to learn what it means to find my joy in God instead of my futile attempts to find joy in someone or something else. He saw the "me" who was becoming who I really am in Christ and by the Spirit—to the glory of the Father.

I am becoming the person God made me to be.

CHAPTER THREE

So What Happened to Me?

≈

For I am not ashamed of the gospel, for it is the power of God for salvation to everyone who believes... Romans 1:16

"What changed you?" I was out on a bike ride with my friend Satish. He had read an early draft of the first chapters of this book and asked the big question — what happened to me? It was a question I had been pondering.

Over the years, I had often sought a deeper spiritual experience. I read books, took courses, prayed, and attended conferences on how to experience spiritual renewal. At one time I had worked through a workbook on how to experience God, only to come away frustrated: it didn't seem to make much difference for me. Patricia and I once attended a conference about spiritual renewal, and we both came away disappointed that it didn't seem to affect us much. For forty-five years I sought a deeper experience of God, too often with frustration and disappointment.

And then, one winter day, I prayed for an hour and my life began to transform. Since that day, I've been thinking about, pondering, and wondering — "What happened?"

A Spiritual Starting Point

The simple explanation for what happened to me in 2017 would be that I came "to know God, or rather to be known by God..."

(Galatians 4:9). I wondered if perhaps, on that day in 2017, I came to genuine faith in Jesus. Could it be that my spiritual beginning, my "conversion" back in 1971, had not been genuine — that my faith had not been real?

In 1971, I began attending Stetson University in Deland, Florida to study accounting. During that first year of college, I began to wrestle with the big questions, the ultimate questions, which are inevitably and unavoidably religious, theological questions. I had always believed in God, but simply believing in God is not enough. There are questions one must ask: *How do we know that there is a God? How do we come to know God? What is life about? Is there ultimate purpose? Is the Bible true?*

Because Stetson was a Baptist university, each student was required to take a religion class for one semester. Though I was an accounting major, I went beyond the requirement, taking a religion class each of the three semesters I was at Stetson. I was so interested in religious questions that one of the religion professors, Earl Joiner, asked me to consider becoming his student assistant, though for reasons that are not clear to me, that never transpired.

During my first semester at Stetson, I began to date my sister's friend, Sharon. I thought things were going well until she told me that she could not continue to see me because I was not a Christian. This was news to me; after all, I went to church! I believed in God! I was moral!

I remember going out, very depressed, and shooting baskets in nearby Lauderdale-by-the-Sea. I went home and called Sharon and expressed an interest in understanding why she didn't think I was a Christian. She took me to a Bible study intended for high school students called the *Northeast Youth Ranch* (it was called "Ranch" though no actual ranching was involved). What most impressed me was how the leaders and students accepted me and genuinely cared for me—which was very attractive to an introvert who struggled with relationships. I believe that God used Sharon and the care of the people at Ranch to lead me into a relationship with himself. While Sharon later broke up with me again, I continued to attend the Bible study.

At Ranch, they talked about the "gospel." Of course, I had heard the word before. I knew that there were "Gospels" in the Bible and that there was something called "gospel" music. But I didn't understand that the word "gospel" means "good news" and is used in the Bible to describe the good news of salvation.

One day one of the girls at Bible study asked someone else whether a certain person was "saved." That just sounded weird to me. What does it mean to be "saved"? Saved from what? I was too shy to ask what she meant, but I eventually began to understand that the gospel was the good news that a person could be saved from the guilt and penalty of their sins.

I also heard the word "grace" a lot at Ranch. "Grace" was usually used in opposition to the word "works." I had heard of the "grace of God" in church, and I had a vague idea of what good works were, but I had never thought about how the two terms related to each other. But that summer I learned that one is saved by grace and not by works. I learned that grace was God's unmerited favor and that salvation was by grace alone, not by things we do in order to earn God's favor.

That freshman year at Stetson was a spiritual starting point for me. I don't know exactly when it happened, but at some point, during that first year of college, I passed, as the Bible says, from spiritual death to spiritual life (1 John 3:14). I said "yes" to Jesus. I came to know God.

Whatever happened to me in 2017, it was not my spiritual beginning as a Christian. My coming to faith in Christ in 1971 was genuine. So, what happened in 2017?

A Spiritual Turning Point

If what happened to me in 2017 was not a conversion experience, what was it? Here is what I have come to think: in 1971 my faith was genuine, but my understanding of the gospel was deficient. In 1971, I understood how to become a Christian through the gospel; in 2017, I came to understand what it means to live through the gospel.

Somehow, in my earliest years as a Christian, I gained the impression that while one could not be saved by good works, once a person was saved by grace he then lived by good works. Grace was how one became a Christian, but it was works that kept one in good standing with God. Saved by faith, live by works—that's what I thought.

I now understand that it is possible to *become* a Christian yet not *live* as a Christian—at least not in the fullness God desires. It is possible to believe the gospel of grace and yet, at the same time, attempt to live a gospel of works. Believing in Jesus is a beginning, but only a beginning. To live as a Christian, we must believe in and rely upon Jesus moment by moment. It is possible to go to church, read the Bible, try hard to live out one's Christianity, and even be a pastor (and perhaps even a successful pastor), but not live the gospel!

I became a Christian using the operating system of grace, but then I sought to live using the operating system of works. Because of my lack of understanding, I failed to experience the gospel power that God intended for me.

The year 2017 was a spiritual turning point.

A Gospel Awakening

My best explanation for 2017 is that sometimes God, in his grace, grants a spiritual experience that is a quantum leap forward in the Christian life.[8] The Christian life is most often a gradual process of growth, a growing awareness of the gospel. But sometimes God gives a breakthrough moment. What happened to me in 2017 was not "conversion" in the sense of the beginning of the Christian journey, but rather a conversion from daily living out of my own resources to learning more and more to live out of gospel resources. It was a conversion from a daily works system to a daily grace system. Author Dane Ortlund calls this a "post-conversion discovery of the gospel."[9] It was the rediscovery of the gospel not just as a doctrine to be believed but as a life to be lived. I discovered that the gospel is not just how you get into Christianity but how you live out Christianity once you are in it.

What happened to me in 2017 was the gospel. I experienced a gospel awakening.

---

[8] The phrase "quantum leap" comes from Jared C. Wilson, *Gospel Wakefulness* (Wheaton, IL: Crossway, 2011), 28.

[9] Dane C. Ortlund, *Deeper: Real Change for Real Sinners* (Wheaton, IL: Crossway, 2021), 107.

I sought to explain to my church what had happened to me in this excerpt from a sermon that was preached two months after my prayer experience in February 2017:

I became more aware of the presence of God. [As I became] more focused on Christ, I asked, myself, "What is this I am feeling? Oh, that must be joy." I have found a new boldness for living—a love that I didn't have before. I have become more aware of the presence of God. I have come to love Jesus more. I believe it is the Holy Spirit: the filling of the Spirit. I am sure that I had experienced the filling of the Holy Spirit in the past, but I have discovered there is a new level of spiritual living.

Perhaps that is a good way to put it. My life before was not devoid of spiritual growth, but in February 2017 I discovered a new level of living.

Why didn't I experience such a change before 2017? Why not 1971, 1980, or 1995? Why would God give me this "quantum leap" forward at the age of 63? My ministry was seemingly coming to an end. At a time when I should have been winding down, I instead felt like I was just beginning. How much better it would have been, I have thought, if God had allowed me to have such an experience 20 years earlier. I don't really know the answer, but perhaps God wanted to paint the wonder of his grace on the canvas of my failure for your sake—so that you might experience his renewing power and presence in your story.

Where Are You on Your Spiritual Journey?[10]

All of us are on this journey called life, and the most important aspect of that journey is the spiritual aspect. So, where are you on your spiritual journey? The Christian experience begins with understanding the gospel. The word 'gospel' means good news. What is this gospel, this good news? The gospel is the transforming message that through faith in Jesus Christ, we enter into and begin to live life as it ought to be. God created us to live in moment by moment relationship with himself. But sin entered our world, breaking that moment by moment relationship. We see the consequences of this brokenness all around us but also in us. We are broken people living in a broken world.

What is the answer to the brokenness of our world? Neither politics nor technology nor all our good efforts can mend our brokenness. Rescue must come from beyond us.

And it does! The good news is that God, in his love, sent Jesus, his Son, to set us free from ourselves, from the penalty of our sin, and from self-destruction. Jesus lived for us, died for us, and rose from the dead for us. Through faith in him, we begin to be made whole. Through faith in him, we can begin to live life as it ought to be lived. Through faith in him, we always have a bright future.

Faith is trust. We must trust Jesus with our time and eternity. What does this trust look like? Suppose that while hiking I come to a very narrow walking bridge over a very deep and wide chasm. I look down… and it is a long way down. I look at the bridge and it is very narrow and very long. The bridge over the chasm swings a bit

---

[10] I learned to ask this question from the lead pastor of my church, Pastor Mike Hearon.

in the wind. What would it mean for me to trust in this bridge? Perhaps I know something about this bridge; that it was built by the finest engineers to hold far more weight than my 170 pounds. I believe that the bridge will hold my weight. I believe it really will take someone across the chasm. In fact, I watch others walk across the bridge successfully. If someone were to ask me if the bridge was safe to walk across, I would respond, "Of course!" All of that is good, of course, but I only express genuine trust the moment I take the first step onto the bridge and begin walking across the chasm.

What is the first step in *life as it ought to be*? It is taking the risky step of trusting in Jesus as Savior and Lord. It is humbling ourselves, turning away from our brokenness, and believing in Jesus. It is declaring we belong to him and then following in his footsteps. We declare ourselves and our faith through the public sign the Bible calls baptism.[11] Baptism isn't conversion but represents a public declaration of being united to Jesus Christ. This declared faith is the first step on the spiritual journey.

The Bible says about this step of faith, "For by grace you have been saved through faith. And this is not your own doing; it is the gift of God, not a result of works, so that no one may boast." (Ephesians 2:8-9).

The pride that is within us cries, "Don't do it! Don't humble yourself! Don't believe!" But the Spirit of God cries, "Believe and

---

[11] Good churches have different views on baptism in relation to faith. My own view is that baptism should always follow faith—it is how we declare our faith. Some churches believe that those who were baptized as infants do not need to be baptized after they come to faith. Discuss with the pastor of a church that believes and teaches the Bible whether you need to be baptized.

you will live! Believe, and you will begin to experience *life as it ought to be.*" The choice is yours.

Have you taken this first step? Have you declared your faith? Without this first step *life as it ought to be* (the topic of the rest of the book) will not be possible. Stop now and ask yourself where you are on your spiritual journey. And if you have not taken the first step of faith in Jesus, ask yourself, "Am I ready to believe in Jesus?" If you are, tell Jesus in prayer. You can declare your faith through prayer like this (in your own words):

> Lord, I have sinned against you. I am not worthy of your love and grace. But I believe that Jesus lived for me, died for me, and rose for me. I believe in him. I want to turn from my sins and declare him to be my Lord and my Savior. Today, I declare my faith! Thank you for forgiveness and a life worth living. Amen.

Perhaps you have already taken the first step: you have believed in Jesus and declared him to be the Lord of your life. You, too, need to ask the question, "Where am I on my spiritual journey?" Are you living the abundant life that Jesus promised (John 10:10)? Do you experience "joy that is inexpressible and filled with glory" (1 Peter 1:8)? Are you filled with "all the fullness of God" (Ephesians 3:19)? Stepping into that supernatural life is what the rest of this book is about.

So, where are you on your spiritual journey?

PART TWO

Ongoing Spiritual Awakening

❧

God can awaken us in a moment. The challenge is to live a life of ongoing spiritual awakening moment by moment, day by day, and more and more. This part of the book seeks to shed light on the gospel path into such ongoing Spirit-filled awakening. Welcome to the adventure of *life as it ought to be*.

CHAPTER FOUR

Living the *Gospel Way*

≈

"Enter by the narrow gate. For the gate is wide and the way is easy that leads to destruction, and those who enter by it are many. For the gate is narrow and the way is hard that leads to life, and those who find it are few." Matthew 7:13,14

As I have said, I began to experience panic attacks in August 2002. I remember a low point: my wife and I were shopping in a Barnes & Noble bookstore. Or rather, she was shopping. I sat in a chair almost catatonic, unable to function. I lost my appetite during that time. I think I was suffering from what is called clinical depression. I felt like I was losing everything. Although I have often struggled with low levels of depression, this was the only time I remember experiencing depression to that degree. In the years that followed I went to multiple counselors, twice went to a retreat for clergy in crisis, took medication (which helped me sleep but did not relieve my anxiety), and read countless books on anxiety. Yet, I continued to experience panic.

Many sought to help me but none (or at least none that I can remember) identified my primary problem: I was not captured by the glory of God but was rather seeking my own glory. I was not satisfied with the wonder of God but was seeking my satisfaction in ministerial success and the approval of others. I was seeking my own glory. Seeking your own glory is stressful. The unrelenting stress of comparing myself with others, living for the approval of people, feeling the need to be successful, and the continual sense of drivenness and hurry was anxiety-producing. The note-free sermon of that particular Sunday in 2002 just pushed me over the edge.

What I believe happened in 2017 was that, in the words of the apostle Paul, I beheld the glory of the Lord. "And we all, with unveiled face, beholding the glory of the Lord, are being transformed into the same image from one degree of glory to another..." (2 Corinthians 3:18).

What is this glory? Paul Tripp tells us that, God's glory is:

> ...God's greatness, beauty, and perfection in all that he is. In everything that he is, God is great beyond human description... It is the stunning reality that there exists one in the universe who is the greatest, the most beautiful, and the most perfect in every way. He is gloriously great, he is gloriously beautiful, and he is gloriously perfect. There is no one like him...[12]

What, then, does it mean to behold the glory of the Lord? It is to see with the eyes of faith the wonder, beauty, and awe of God. When you behold his glory, you are set free from the desire to glorify yourself, and you do not need the approval of others. The only thing that can make sense of our twisted world is a fresh vision of the glory of God.

An Ongoing Experience of the Glory of God

In the months following my life-changing encounter with God's glory, I asked the question that I continue to wrestle with: "Can I

---

[12] Paul David Tripp, *Do You Believe?: 12 Historic Doctrines to Change Your Everyday Life* (Wheaton, IL: Crossway, 2021), 70.

continue to experience this spiritual awakening day by day?" I didn't want to return to my old way of thinking and living.

Sometime later, my brother asked me: "Is what happened to you something you can teach others?" In the almost seven years since that sacred moment of 2017, I have been pondering those two questions. Put as one question: "How can I or others experience ongoing spiritual awakening?"

I have come to believe that ongoing spiritual awakening is to be the normal way for God's people. We are always to be awake to the beauty and wonder of God. We must continually behold the glory of God if we want to live transformed lives. But beholding the glory of God is more than an intellectual exercise. It is more than attending church, reading the Bible, saying the occasional prayer, and avoiding the big sins. It is and must be a moment by moment, day by day experience of God's glory. We need an experiential encounter with the glory of God if we are to live well. We need God to reveal himself to us, perhaps as he did to me. But this is frustrating. How can I get God to reveal himself to me? The answer is that God continually reveals himself to those who have eyes to see and ears to hear. He reveals himself in the creation, in the Scripture, and by the Spirit who lives in us. Creation, Scripture, and the Spirit all testify to the glory of God revealed "in the face of Jesus Christ" (2 Corinthians 4:6). Our responsibility is to seek him continually (Psalm 105:4), to continually set our minds on things above (Colossians 3:1-2), to continually offer our bodies as living sacrifices (Romans 12:1), to continually look to the unseen things (2 Corinthians 4:18), and then to continually trust that God will reveal himself in accordance with his good purposes.

This book began with my story. But it is about more than my story. It is about your story, and it is about *the* story, the story of God's glory and grace. *You don't need my experience, but you do need my reality.* You need the reality of beholding the glory of God. The rest of the book is about how we experience the glory of God amidst the stress and busyness of life in a broken world.

Life As It Ought to Be

I call a life of ongoing awakening to the beauty and wonder of God *life as it ought to be,* life as God intends. *Life as it ought to be* is about experiencing life the way God wants you to experience it: a life of fullness in a world of emptiness, a life of wholeness in a world of brokenness, and a life of joy in a joyless world. *Life as it ought to be* is about beholding the glory of God. Paul describes this life in his great prayer in Ephesians 3:14-21.

> [14]For this reason I bow my knees before the Father, [15]from whom every family in heaven and on earth is named, [16]that according to the **riches of his glory** he may grant you to be **strengthened with power through his Spirit** in your inner being, [17]so that **Christ may dwell in your hearts** through faith—that you, being rooted and grounded in love, [18]may have strength to comprehend with all the saints what is the breadth and length and height and depth, [19]and to know the love of Christ that surpasses knowledge, that you may be **filled with all the fullness of God**. [20]Now to him who is able to do far more abundantly than all that we ask or think, according to the power at work within us, [21]**to him be glory** in the church and in Christ Jesus throughout all generations, forever and ever. Amen.

This prayer is not a wish that won't be fulfilled or an ideal that can never be realized. It is a prayer that all of God's people can and should experience. It is a prayer that we might pursue his glory, that we might experience his power, and that we might be aware of his presence—with the ultimate goal of "being filled with all the fullness of God," as the highlighted portions above indicate.

Life as it ought to be is not a program but a supernatural awakening by the Spirit. It is not a mechanical formula but a power-filled approach to supernatural living. It is not three steps to a better life but a path that takes us toward the life God intends.

What Keeps Us from Living Life As It Ought to Be?

If *life as it ought to be* is God's plan for his people, why is it that, too often, believers do not live this supernatural life? The simple answer is that we are blinded by our sin, particularly the sin of pride. Our pride blinds us to the depth of our sin and inadequacy. Christians still live in a broken world, and we continue to live under the influence of the power of sin. Instead of looking to the unseen things, we look to the seen things (2 Corinthians 4:18); instead of seeking the things above, we seek the things of this world (Colossians 3:1-2). We allow the busyness of life to distract us from the things that matter most. We are infected with the "nice life syndrome." And thus, we fail to see the beauty and wonder and majesty of God that surrounds us every moment. Our pride and sin distract us from what matters most: the glory of God.

My daughter Megan and I have taken up scuba diving together. Recently, we went on a dive trip. On this particular day, I was having scuba problems: my mask leaked, I was having problems equalizing the pressure in my ears, I was underweighted and had a problem staying submerged, and I had lost my camera. Let's just say I was having a bad scuba day. From time to time when we were on the surface, Megan would ask me, "Did you see the beautiful fish?" or "Did you see that wonderful sight?" The answer each time was "No, I didn't see it." I was distracted by my scuba problems.

The problems of our lives are real. But when our lives are consumed not only with the problems and responsibilities of life but with social media, on-demand entertainment, year-round sports, and 24-hour newsfeeds, Word and prayer are pushed to the periphery of our living, and we fail to behold his glory.

Beholding His Glory

A while back a friend asked me the right question: "Where do I begin?" We must begin with God and his glory. My story of renewal began with seeing more clearly the majesty and wonder of our magnificent God. Out of my struggle, joylessness, and frustration (see Chapter 1), I caught a glimpse of glory. My only hope to continue to experience awakening is to see the glory and beauty of God day by day.

We need more than a theoretical knowledge of God's glory; we need a disruptive encounter with the glory of God—every day! These encounters might be of the "I was blind but now I see" variety (John 9:25). They might be small nudges of the Spirit through the Word of God or the encouragement of a friend, but we need such encounters each day. If the gospel does not disrupt our living, we are not hearing it well. When the gospel is not experienced, the gospel is not lived. How do we encounter the glory of God each day? We must walk the *gospel way*.

The Gospel Way

We behold his glory as we live the *gospel way*. The gospel is the path into life and the path of life. It is the lens that enables us to see the glory of God "in the face of Jesus Christ" (2 Corinthians 4:6). A couple of definitions will help.

Gospel — The word gospel means "good news." In ancient times, a victorious army would send a messenger to their homeland with the "gospel" of their victory: the good news of a great triumph. I call the gospel of Jesus the "best news possible," the story of ultimate victory. What is the good news of Jesus—this gospel? The gospel is the transforming message that through faith in Jesus Christ, we enter into and begin to live *life as it ought to be*. It is through faith that we become united to Jesus and his death and resurrection. It is through faith that we step into this new life and it is through faith that we begin to live this new life.

What does it mean to live the *Gospel Way* — Living the *gospel way* can be expressed in a sentence: *Gospel power unleashed in three gospel practices produces gospel-awakened people.* Gospel power is the *essence* of walking the *gospel way*. Gospel practices are the *means* of living the *gospel way*. Gospel awakening is the *fruit* of living the *gospel way*.

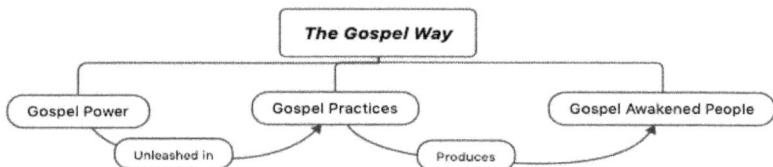

The Gospel Way

Gospel Power	Gospel Practices	Gospel Awakened People
Unleashed in	Produces	

The rest of this second section of the book will seek to explain the details of this path into life as it should be.

To live the *gospel way,* we must live *"polepole"*—a Swahili word that my daughter and I learned from our scuba diving guides on a recent trip to Zanzibar. It is translated "slowly, slowly." In scuba diving, slower is better. When you hurry, you use up your air faster (usually my problem) and, most importantly, you miss the glory that surrounds you. To behold his glory, we must learn to slow down and see.

As a pastor, I was usually in a hurry. I had to make things happen, and this did not serve me well. On that day in February 2017, I prayed for an extended time. This meant slowing down—putting aside email, reading, and other tasks—and focusing on God and his Word. For me, this was the path to beholding his glory.

A Mystery to Be Lived

The path I am going to recommend in these next chapters is not a mechanical process with guaranteed scientific results, nor is it a wish that may only be attained by the few. It is a mystery to be lived by all God's people. The essence of my experience with God was communion with God, but this communion is not for just a few of God's people. All of God's people now have access to God through Jesus. In Romans 5:1-2 Paul tells us, "Therefore, since we have been justified by faith, we have peace with God through our Lord Jesus Christ. Through him we have also obtained *access* by faith into this grace in which we stand..." (emphasis added). All those justified by faith have access into the grace of God—we always have access to God himself. Walking in this moment by moment communion is what I call *life as it ought to be.* The *gospel way* is the path toward this transforming communion.

The *gospel way* is a mystery that cannot be fully understood, yet it can be lived. It is the mystery of experiencing union with Jesus, walking in the power of the Spirit, and pursuing the Father's agenda moment by moment, day by day, and more and more.

Living the Supernatural

Living the gospel is a supernatural journey. In my last years of ministry at our church in New Jersey, I often reminded my congregation that the Christian life is to be supernatural. I was not suggesting that the natural world doesn't exist but rather that the Christian always lives simultaneously in the realms of the natural and the supernatural. The Christian life is always to be lived in the supernatural power of the Spirit.

It is helpful to distinguish between the *ordinary supernatural work of the Spirit* and *the extraordinary supernatural work of the Spirit.* The ordinary supernatural work of the Spirit is loving our neighbors as ourselves, being patient with one another, and putting others before ourselves. All of that is a supernatural work of the Spirit. The extraordinary supernatural work of the Spirit is what we usually call miracles. Miracles, by definition, are rare. Most of this book is about how we live in the ordinary supernatural work of the Spirit moment by moment and day by day.

That said, sometimes God gives glimpses of the extraordinary supernatural work of his Spirit. In the next few chapters, I have included what I call "Glimpses of Glory." "Glimpses of Glory are extraordinary stories of God's power and presence. They are intended to remind us that we are always to live in God's supernatural power.

A Glimpse of Glory — Dan's Story

An apparent healing episode in a medical practice.

As a practicing physician for over 30 years, I have had a few patients apparently miraculously recover from disease. The most remarkable episode involved an individual who was paralyzed due to an accident. At the time I began to care for him, he had been in a wheelchair for some years. He had seen other physicians and had been cared for in a rehab hospital due to the accident, and there was no question of his diagnosis. I came into the office one day and saw him as I was walking in. He called to me and said, "Hey Doc, look!" and then stood up from the waiting room chair—no longer in a wheelchair and standing easily.

In my shock and delight I asked him to immediately come back to an exam room to tell me what had happened. This is his story:

He attended a local church that actively believed in and practiced healing prayer. They designated certain people to be on a team that prayed for healing, and he served on one of those teams. One of the members recognized the paradox of this and suggested they pray for him. He obviously agreed, and they gathered around him to pray. As they placed their hands on him and prayed, he said that he felt "like his legs were on fire" and he stood upright on his previously paralyzed legs. He not only stood but walked and kept walking. He no longer had mobility limitations and, in a fairly short period of time, became the floor manager of a large store in the area where he lived. While at work he was on his feet constantly, walking the floor. The store closed some years ago and he and his wife moved from the area, but I know that God does still heal paralytics even in our day. I know because I have seen a paralyzed man walk.

CHAPTER FIVE

Gospel Power

≈

For me to live is Christ... Philippians 1:21

I remember once, sometime after February 2017, arranging to meet someone who was new to the church at Panera Bread near where I lived in Piscataway. I don't remember all that we talked about—his life, our church, etc. But afterward, as I walked back to my car, I remember thinking, "Was that me?" Ordinarily, in situations like that, I would play the pastoral role, worrying about what the other person would think, focused on saying the "right" thing—wholly self-conscious. But there was none of that this time. I was unaware of myself; I didn't worry about what he would think of me in the future. I was conscious, not of myself, but of the person I was talking to and the God whose gospel I was seeking to convey. For me, that was the transforming power of the gospel.

The Power of the Gospel

It is in the gospel that we experience the power of God. The gospel is the power of God for salvation (Romans 1:16). In 2 Corinthians 4:7, the apostle Paul calls the gospel "the surpassing power." The gospel is the power that rescues us from condemnation and the gospel is the power that enables us to live a new life. I love how Paul puts it in Ephesians 1:19-20 when he speaks of "the immeasurable greatness of his power toward us who believe, according to the working of his great might that he worked in Christ when he raised him from the dead and seated him at his right hand in the heavenly places…" Gospel power is greater than any earthly power, and this is the power that is available every day to those who believe in Jesus. This power flows from our union with Jesus and is lived out by the empowerment of the Holy Spirit as we seek God's purpose for us.

Our Powerlessness

The truth we hide from ourselves is that too often we live powerless lives devoid of any genuine sense of the presence and purpose of God. Too often we live with a theoretical knowledge of the gospel when what we need is a lived experience of gospel power. Christians who live without the power-filled presence of the gospel are like a cruise ship that lost power after one of its two engines was destroyed in a fire. While the second engine was fully capable of powering the ship—a ship that had plenty of fuel—the line that connected the control room with the power ran through the engine room that had been disabled by the fire—meaning that the connecting line had also been destroyed by fire. The ship had plenty of available power, but it had lost connection with the source of its power, and so it was "dead in the water," stranding its many passengers in the process. Too often we lose connection to our power source, the gospel of Jesus Christ. We are spiritually "dead in the water." Living the *gospel way* is how we connect with the power of the gospel.

Three Aspects of Gospel Power

This gospel power has three aspects: living *in Christ, by the Spirit,* and *to the glory of the Father.* These three are interdependent aspects of living the gospel.

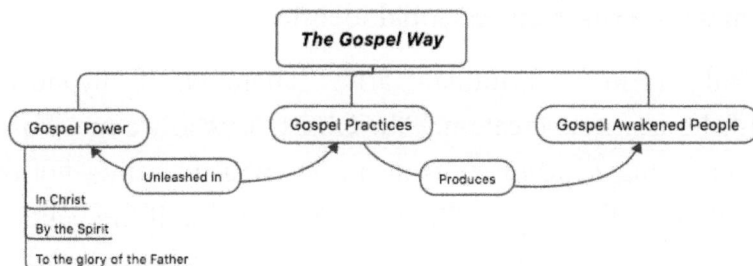

In Christ

One of the more important theological truths found in Scripture is the doctrine of our union with Jesus. Union with Jesus is one of the apostle Paul's most-loved concepts. Altogether he used the phrases "in Christ," "in Christ Jesus," "in the Lord," and "in him" approximately 164 times in his letters.[13] Here are a few examples:

- "So, you also must consider yourselves dead to sin and alive to God in Christ Jesus." Romans 6:11

- "There is neither Jew nor Greek, there is neither slave nor free, there is no male and female, for you are all one in Christ Jesus." Galatians 3:28

- In Ephesians 1:3-14, Paul uses the expressions "in Christ," "in him," and "in the beloved" a combined nine times.

But what does it mean to be "in Christ" or "in Jesus"? I suggest two related ideas.

---

[13] Marcus Johnson, *One with Christ: An Evangelical Theology of Salvation* (Wheaton, IL: Crossway, 2013), 19.

Union with Jesus is our essential identity

Paul says in 2 Corinthians 5:17, "Therefore, if anyone is in Christ, he is a new creation." "In Christ" is who we are. For the believer, being *in Jesus* is his or her essential identity—not race, occupation, nationality, politics, or anything else. If the believer is asked to explain who she is, the first thing that comes to mind should be, "I am in Christ." On good days and bad days and in-between days, the believer is *in Christ*; he or she belongs to him. To live the gospel, we must remember who we are—we are in Christ!

Union with Jesus is also to be our experiential reality

In Galatians 2:20, Paul declares, "I have been crucified with Christ. It is no longer I who live, but Christ who lives in me. And the life I now live in the flesh I live by faith in the Son of God, who loved me and gave himself for me." Union with Jesus is not simply who we are; it is how we live life. Union with Jesus is more than a doctrine to be understood; it is an experience to be had. Richard Lovelace reminds us, "Spiritual life flows out of union with Christ, not merely imitation of Christ."[14] Adam Neder tells us that our subjective response to the gospel is "how we become (in ourselves) who we already are (in Christ)."[15]

To live in union with Jesus is to live in union with his cross and resurrection (see Romans 6:1-11). This means that we somehow participate in the cross and resurrection. But how do we do that? As Jesus died for our sins, we die to our sins. The Bible calls this

---

[14] Richard Lovelace, *Dynamics of Spiritual Life: An Evangelical Theology of Renewal* (Downers Grove, IL: InterVarsity Press, 1979), 74.

[15] Adam Neder, *Theology As a Way of Life: On Teaching and Learning the Christian Faith* (Grand Rapids: Baker Academic, 2019), 26.

repentance, a recognition of our specific sin and a turning away from specific sins. But we also participate in his resurrection. As Jesus rose from physical death, we rise to newness of life each day. In union with Jesus, we begin to live a new way (2 Corinthians 5:17), the *gospel way*. The presence of the gospel is experienced as we are united to him in his cross and resurrection.

Here is an imaginative illustration: suppose that I am an artist who paints. I consider myself a good painter; in fact, I am quite proud of my painting. My hero is the great painter Gerhard Richter (who, I have read, is the world's most famous living painter). Suppose I am invited to visit Gerhard Richter in his studio, and I go. I see the beauty of his art, I watch with wonder as he paints, and I am in awe. As I watch the master paint, as I behold the beauty of his work, suddenly I realize that I am not nearly as good a painter as I thought I was. I see flaws in my painting that I had never noticed before. All my painting now seems like the scribblings of a young child. I realize that I will never be a painter like Gerhard Richter. I am not able.

But then—stick with me here—Richter says to me, "It is possible if you will allow it, for me to take up residence within you and to paint with you and through you. You will still be painting, but as you participate in me and I in you, you will paint better than you ever thought possible." That imaginative story illustrates union with Jesus. Christ is in us, and we are in Christ, and he now lives through us.

But how?

How do we live this union with Jesus? What needs to happen so that at the end of a day we can say, "Today I lived in union with Jesus"?

To live in union with Jesus we must intentionally see the wonder of his glory, experience the depth of our failure and inability, and then embrace the wonder of Christ in us. This enables us to live beyond what we are able. Paul expresses this truth in Colossians 1:29: "For this I toil, struggling with all his energy that he powerfully works within me."

As I recently walked my daughter's dog Jesse on the path along the Savannah River near our home, I stopped to talk to some new friends, Jack and Marcie. We talked about the weather and our plans for the day, but eventually, our conversation turned to the gospel. I asked them "What does it mean for us to live in union with Jesus today?" Marcie's answer was both simple and profound: "Believe it and live it." Exactly! We need to *believe* that we are united to Jesus (our essential identity) and to *live* as those united to Jesus (our lived reality). To live *in Christ* then is to live with an awareness of Jesus in us.

Remind yourself as often as you can that you are to live *in Christ.*

By the Spirit

The second aspect of gospel living is relying upon the empowerment of the Spirit. The Holy Spirit has been given to us to empower us to live a new life. The Old Testament promised the coming of the Spirit; we now live in the age of fulfillment. The Spirit has been given. We are no longer to live in our own strength but in the power of the Holy Spirit. In the Old Testament, certain people (mostly prophets, priests, and kings) were empowered by the Spirit. Zechariah 4:6 provides this guidance for one of the leaders of God's people: "This is the word of the LORD to Zerubbabel: Not by might, nor by power, but by my Spirit, says the LORD of hosts." But now, in this age of fulfillment, all of God's people are to live in the power of the Holy Spirit (Acts 2:17-18). Each of us is to be empowered by the Spirit.

I received this email from a man in our church in Spring, 2017: "I wanted to comment on last week's sermon. It was among the best I've ever heard you give. The content was solid… but there was something different about your delivery. You were vulnerable but confident. Maybe it was your body language, or the topic, or what you had for breakfast—I'm not sure. But you were definitely 'in the zone.'" I responded: "Thanks for the encouraging words. I think it was the Holy Spirit. That's my story, and I'm sticking to it…" Years later, I see no need to change that story.

I have begun to discover, in the months and years following 2017, what it means to "walk by the Spirit" and to "…keep in step with the Spirit."[16] The Holy Spirit is the third person of the Trinity. It is through the Holy Spirit that the power of the gospel is experienced. The Holy Spirit is the one who fills us (Ephesians 3:19; 5:18), guides us (Acts 13:1-4; Luke 4:1), empowers us for newness of life (Galatians 5:16-26), and empowers us for ministry (Acts 1:8). In Ephesians 3:16, Paul prays that "…according to the riches of his glory he may grant you to be strengthened with power through his Spirit in your inner being."

---

[16] Galatians 5:16, 25.

If we have Jesus in us, you may ask, then why do we need the Spirit? We need the Spirit because the Spirit is the one who applies the gospel (Christ in us) to our hearts and lives. The Spirit is the one who unites us to Jesus. And the Spirit is the one who unleashes gospel power into our living.

We need the Spirit as Jesus needed the Spirit.[17] When Jesus was among us he temporarily put aside the expressions of his divine power and glory. In Luke 4, one of the passages that describes the temptation of Jesus, we are told Jesus was "full of the Holy Spirit" (v. 1), was "led by the Spirit" (v. 1), and went "in the power of the Spirit" (v. 14). Jesus lived and ministered by the power of the Holy Spirit. If Jesus lived in the power of the Spirit, how much more do I need to live by the power of the Spirit?

But how?

How, then, do we live in the power of the Spirit? In Galatians 5:16, Paul tells us to "walk by the Spirit." To walk by the Spirit is to rely upon the Spirit's power and guidance, which enable us to live better than we are able to live in our own strength! To walk by the Spirit is to expect the Spirit to guide and empower us each day. To walk by the Spirit is to (1) be aware of our own inadequacy, (2) intentionally rely upon the Spirit, and (3) make every effort as we seek to further the Spirit's purposes.

What does this look like? The best illustration I can think of is the writing of this book. As I write, I am very aware of my inadequacy. Perhaps I could write an interesting book through my

---

[17] See Gerald F. Hawthorne, *The Presence and the Power: The Significance of the Holy Spirit in The Life and Ministry of Jesus* (Eugene, OR: Wipf and Stock Publishers, 1991).

own resources, but to write a book that will help people to live life in the power of the gospel is beyond my ability.

Because I am aware of my inadequacy, I have been seeking to intentionally rely upon the Spirit of God to work in me and through me. Just now I prayed, "Holy Spirit, help me as I write." Yet, at the same time, I have been making every effort and using all the resources I have to attempt to write well. Writing a book, I have discovered, is hard work. I originally thought this book would be finished in six months—that was four years ago! I have written and rewritten—again and again, assisted by many people who have given me thoughts and insights. I have no idea how many hours I have invested in writing this short book.

I don't consider myself a great writer. Writing often seems difficult for me. But just now, as I'm engaged in editing this book, I thought to myself, "This is better than I am able!" When we walk by the Spirit, we find ourselves living better than we are able.

In all of life we are to live expecting to experience the power of the Spirit. Remind yourself as often as you can that you are to live *in Christ* and *by the Spirit.*

To the Glory of the Father

The third aspect of the life of faith is seeking God's glory, not our glory. Christians of all sorts recognize the glory of God as the ultimate end of all things. We often append our prayers with "for your glory." But too often, we don't understand in any practical sense what it means to live for God's glory and not for our own. We fail to realize that to live for God's glory means giving up our own agendas.

When we seek our own agendas, we are seeking our own glory. To seek God's glory then is to give up pursuing our agendas and to begin to seek God's better agenda—for his glory. The Christian life orientation is found in Psalm 115:1, "Not to us, O LORD, not to us, but to your name give glory..." When I live for the glory of God, I give up my "nice life" plans and step into God's "better life" plans.

This basic truth is also found in the Lord's Prayer, "Our Father in heaven, hallowed be your name. Your kingdom come, your will be done, on earth as it is in heaven" (Matthew 6:9-10). The Lord's Prayer is, first of all, a prayer for God's glory ("hallowed be your name"). But to pray for God's glory means that we must desire his kingdom to come (not ours) and for his will to be done (not ours). To seek the Father's glory, then, is to give up our agendas in specific ways.

This truth is exemplified later in Matthew's Gospel, in Jesus' passionate prayer in the Garden of Gethsemane: "My Father, if it be possible, let this cup pass from me; nevertheless, not as I will, but as you will" (Matthew 26:39). Jesus was in agony, knowing he would soon suffer while bearing the sins of his people. In his humanity, he did not want to be crucified. But he said "no" to his human desire so that he might embrace the Father's greater agenda. In eternity, we will discover that God's will for us is always better than our will for us.

Our problem is that we want our will to be God's will. We do want God's will, but only if it coincides with what we want. But it doesn't work that way. We must be willing to say "no" to what we desire if we are to discover God's better "yes." Gary Tyra puts it this way: "…the Christian's ultimate concern must be to *please God*."[18] It is okay to have secondary concerns, but those secondary concerns must always flow out of our ultimate concern to please God and to further his agenda.

In 2022 I learned a hard lesson: I must die to *life as I want it to be* if I am to experience *life as it ought to be*. I discovered that God's agenda was not the same as my agenda. One of my retirement ministry ideas (and I had many) was to continue to serve as a Regional Leader with the ministry of the *6:4 Fellowship*[19] and to expand that role in my new phase of life. In October 2021, three months into my retirement, Dennis Henderson, one of the leaders of the *6:4 Fellowship*, called me and asked me to consider serving as the Regional Director for the *6:4 Fellowship*'s Mid-Atlantic Region. Regional Directors oversee the various Regional Leaders in a particular region of the country. The position was supposed to require one day a week, and this proposed ministry seemed a perfect fit. The *6:4 Fellowship* is about prayer and revival, both of which have become my passions.

Dennis invited me to fly to Austin, Texas for a meeting of the Regional Directors, which I did. After that meeting, and because I knew my wife Patricia was hesitant because of my tendency to over-commit, I agreed to serve as an acting Regional Director for several months until the *6:4 Fellowship National Conference* in Katy, Texas, the following March. My thinking: if, after the conference, I had seen fruit from the ministry and Patricia *wanted* me to serve as

---

[18] Gary Tyra, *Introduction to Spirituality: Cultivating a Lifestyle of Faithfulness* (Grand Rapids: Baker Academic, 2023), 37.

[19] The *6:4 Fellowship* is a fellowship of "pastors committed to prayer and word powered ministry." The name is based on Acts 6:4. For more information, see 64fellowship.com.

Regional Director and not simply agreed that it was *okay* for me to serve, then I would do it. I wanted her to be enthusiastic about whatever new ministry role I might take on. Dennis agreed, so that's what I did.

Patricia and I attended the National Conference that March. The week following the conference, knowing that I needed to give Dennis an answer as to whether I would serve as a Regional Director, Patricia and I talked. As we did, it became clear that my wife did not express the level of enthusiasm for this new role for which I had hoped. Still, I managed to convince her and myself that this was a very significant ministry opportunity and that I could make a real contribution and I would keep it to one day a week, etc., etc., etc. I think I may have even said something like, "This may be the most significant ministry I will ever do!" How could she protest that? So, she said, "Okay." While her response was less than the full endorsement I said that I wanted, I went with it. Based on her "okay" response, that afternoon I told Dennis that I would serve as Regional Director for the Mid-Atlantic region. He asked me what Patricia thought, and I told him that she was okay with my decision. And that was that... or so I thought.

The next morning, I awoke and realized that though Patricia had said "okay," Jesus hadn't said "okay." I realized that in accepting the *6:4 Fellowship* position, I was seeking my own glory, not God's glory. I was seeking my own significance, not seeking to demonstrate God's significance. I didn't know it then, but God had a better plan for me. I realized that I had to do something that was difficult for me; I had to call Dennis back and say "no." So that morning I dialed his number and told him that I couldn't do it. I told him that though

Patricia had said "okay," I hadn't told him the full story. He was very affirming of my decision.

After I hung up the phone, I realized that the *6:4 Fellowship* wasn't all that I had to say "no" to. I realized that I needed to say "no," not only to becoming a Regional Director for the *6:4 Fellowship* but also to my whole list of ministry ideas. I had to say "no" to my whole agenda! I needed to die to my agenda. I had to surrender the control of my future. I needed to understand that the greatest obstacle to God's agenda was my agenda!

I went downstairs and told Patricia what I had done. I hadn't told her what I was going to do before calling Dennis—for fear that she would try to talk me out of it. When I told her what I had done—not only saying "no" to the 6:4 Fellowship position but saying "no" to my whole list of ideas—she said she was "stunned"—she even said it twice! She didn't think I was capable of saying "no" to something that I really wanted to do—for her sake. I am not proud of this.

In saying "no" to the *6:4 Fellowship* and to my list of ideas, I was saying "no" to my search for my own glory and significance. I was saying "Not to me, O Lord, not to me, but to your name be glory!" (Psalm 115:1).

As Patricia and I talked and prayed that morning, we decided that for the next months, we would spend time together, seek Jesus together, laugh together, and hear God's voice together. We decided that I would take a sabbatical from any formal ministry commitment as we sought God's agenda for us.

The fruit of seeking his agenda may not always be evident in this world, but from the perspective of eternity, it will be seen that God's agenda is always better than our own.

Two weeks after relaying my "no" decision to Dennis Henderson, my brother Gere wondered aloud what impact turning down this opportunity would have in a year's time. A year later, as I reflected on Gere's question, I could readily see the fruit of that decision. The months of sabbatical flew by. While on a trip to Ireland—the end point of my sabbatical—while walking a lonely but majestic Irish beach, the Lord gave me clarity on the ministry path I believe I should pursue. It seems so much better than all my ministry ideas! If I hadn't said, "no" to my agenda, I couldn't have said "yes" to his much better agenda.[20]

(Derryname Beach in Kerry, Ireland, where I discovered God's better "yes")

---

[20] God's better agenda for me is the ministry I am now leading: *Life As It Ought to Be.*

To live for the glory of the Father, we must say "no" to our agendas so that we can say "yes" to his better agenda. I am learning to cease seeking to do great things for my glory and instead seek to do small things to the glory of a great God. When we live for the glory of the Father, we anticipate the glory that one day we will share with the Father and live in light of the day when we will give account for every word, thought, and action. We anticipate and pursue the purpose of the Father.

Remind yourself as often as you can that you are to live *in Christ, by the Spirit,* and *to the glory of the Father.*

A Trinitarian Approach

Recently, when my brother Gere and I were reading Romans 8:1-18 (a primary text on living the Christian life), he commented on how the Trinity is woven throughout the passage. This is true because the Trinity is woven into the gospel. The Trinity is the Bible's idea that God is one yet exists as three persons: Father, Son, and Holy Spirit. Living *in Christ, by the Spirit, to the glory of the Father* is a Trinitarian approach to gospel living. The gospel is about Jesus but not just Jesus. The Father sent the Son to fulfill his purpose. The Son accomplished salvation. And the Spirit applies this salvation to human hearts. Michael Horton explains that the three persons of the Trinity are always working together: "It is not different works but different *roles* in *every work* that the divine persons perform."[21]

The three persons are at work in our becoming Christians and the three are at work in our living as Christians. The three aspects

---

[21] Michael Horton, *Rediscovering the Holy Spirit: God's Perfecting Presence in Creation, Redemption, and Everyday Life* (Grand Rapids: Zondervan, 2017), 38.

of gospel power are really one life of faith. We can think of it like this: "In Christ" is the *What?* of the gospel; "by the Spirit" is the *How?* of the gospel; and "to the glory of the Father" is the *"Why?"* of the gospel.[22] The three aspects can be thought of separately but cannot be lived separately. When we experience one person of the Trinity, we experience all three aspects even when we are not aware of it. The three are really one. Thus, when I live *in Christ,* I am living *by the Spirit* and *to the glory of the Father.* When I live *by the Spirit,* I am living *in Christ* and *to the glory of the* Father. And when I live *to the glory of the Father,* I am living *in Christ* and *by the Spirit.* Whether consciously or subconsciously, we are to live *in Christ, by the Spirit,* and *for the glory of the Father.* The power of the gospel is experienced as we live out these three aspects of gospel living.

Moment by Moment

This gospel power can only be experienced moment by moment. Theologian Francis Schaeffer puts it this way: "I can only live [the Christian life] in practice one moment at a time... The real solution [to living the Christian life] is being cast up into the moment by moment communion, with God himself, and letting Christ's truth flow through me through the agency of the Holy Spirit... To believe him, not just when I accept Christ as Savior, but every moment, one moment at a time: this is the Christian life, and this is true spirituality."[23]

---

[22] I am indebted to my friend Kathy Davis for this insight.
[23] Francis A. Schaeffer, *True Spirituality* (Wheaton, IL: Tyndale House Publishers, 2001), 77, 79, 80.

It is only possible for us to live in this one moment. The question, then, is *"How* do I live in this one moment?" We can live anxious, frustrated, driven lives in this moment, or we can live this moment walking in the power of the God who created us.

My friend Mike Phillips recently took me mountain biking. I had never been mountain biking before, but I rented a good mountain bike from a local bike shop for the occasion. As we began, I instantly realized that mountain biking is a present-tense adventure. To survive (which I did—just barely!), I had to look at the trail that was immediately before me every moment of the ride. I had to avoid the root or the tree jutting into the trail. I needed to watch for dips and prepare to shift gears for the hill right in front of me. I spent almost no time thinking about what was around the corner because I had no idea what was around the corner. I just followed Mike. I trusted him moment by moment.

That is how we are to experience the Christian life: we never know what is around the corner, so we must stop worrying about what is around the corner. We stay as close to Jesus as we can by the Spirit and for the Father's glory. We must learn to live today as if there is no tomorrow, only venturing into the future for necessary planning and prayer. We must live the power of the gospel in this one moment, trusting God for the unseen moments around the corner. The power of the gospel can only be experienced in this one moment.

The essence of the Christian life is living moment by moment, aware of the presence of Jesus (*in Christ*), expecting the power of his Spirit (*by the Spirit*), and pursuing the Father's glorious purpose (*for the glory of the Father*). Is such a moment by moment life possible? We cannot live this life perfectly, but we can do so increasingly.

Experiential Reality

But we cannot hurry on; we must pause and reflect on the practical question of how we experience, in any one moment, the power of the gospel. Without this experiential reality, the rest of this book becomes an exercise in frustration. What transformed my life in 2017 was not a strategy, a formula, or a new understanding of theology. What transformed me was faith. By faith, I saw, in the Scriptures, the glory of God. By faith, I saw the darkness of my own soul. By faith, I began to live out of my union with Christ. By faith, I learned to rely upon the Spirit for my strength. And by faith, I began to believe that the Father's agenda was better than my agenda. In the days that followed, I began to ask, "Am I in this one moment living by faith in the Father, Son, and Holy Spirit?"

To have faith is to trust. We must transfer our trust from our own human resources and put our trust wholly in our God who is Father, Son, and Spirit. Psalm 20:7 puts it this way, "Some trust in chariots and some in horses, but we trust in the name of the LORD our God."

This life of faith is an active passivity.[24] We are passive as we offer our inadequate selves wholly to God (Romans 12:1). We bring empty hands. But we are also active as we step into this one moment, intentionally trusting in God and his words in the practical realities of life.

---

[24] Schaeffer, *True Spirituality*, 51-53.

To experience the supernatural life that God intends, I must moment by moment trust in God. I must stop trusting in my resources and abilities and intentionally be aware of his presence, rely upon his power, and pursue his agenda. We must have this kind of trust to become a Christian and we must have this kind of trust in order to live as a Christian.

What does this faith look like? I remember going to a hospital to visit a family member of someone who attended our church. This person had been in a very serious automobile accident. I did not expect the woman from my church to be there when I arrived, but I did expect that there would be family members who I did not know. I knew I was capable of saying the wrong thing or simply sounding pastoral without being of much help or comfort to this distressed family—I realized my inadequacy. I wanted the Spirit to speak through me. I wanted to walk the path of the gospel. I wanted the Father to be glorified. Before entering the hospital, I stopped in front of the main doors and said to the Lord and to myself, "In Christ, by the Spirit, to the glory of the Father." I sought to rely upon the power of Jesus, by the Spirit, and for the Father. Then, I did my best to minister to that grieving family, and I think I ministered better than I am able.

"In Christ, by the Spirit, for the glory of the Father" is my way of expressing my trust in Jesus, who is united to me by the Spirit and is at work in me for the glory of the Father. This is the moment by moment life of faith. This is how we experience the power of the gospel.

Supernatural Gospel Mode

I like to think of this moment by moment life of faith as a different mode of being and living. Please allow me to illustrate. I recently bought an E-Bike. My E-Bike is not an electric bike but a peddle-assist bike. You must peddle for the electric power to help you. You can use the bike without the peddle-assist turned on, but it is a heavy bike so it is a slow go, and some hills might be impossible. But peddle with the assist turned on and you can find yourself going faster than you are able by your own power. You still have to peddle, you are still involved—no peddling and you go nowhere—but when you turn on the peddle assist and then peddle, you experience a power that is greater than your own efforts. Hills can still be difficult, and you may still get tired, but with the peddle assist, you are able to persevere even through difficulty. In essence, there are two modes on my bike: manual mode and peddle assist mode.

When my E-Bike is fully charged, the power of the E-Bike is present but is not ready to be used. When I push the button that turns on the peddle-assist, the power is ready to be used but is not yet active. It is when I begin to peddle with the peddle assist turned on that the power of the bike is actually unleashed in my riding. At that moment, I have moved from manual mode to peddle-assist mode, and I ride faster than I am able to ride in my own strength.

Living the *gospel way* is similar. There are two modes in which we can seek to live Christianity: manual mode and supernatural gospel mode. Manual mode is doing our best in our own resources. It is making the best of a difficult situation. Manual mode is trying really hard. But manual mode is a tough go. Too often we get stuck in manual mode.

Supernatural gospel mode is different. When I live *in Christ, by the Spirit, for the glory of the Father,* I align my heart with the power of the gospel. In that one moment, the power of the gospel is ready to be lived. As I rely on Christ working in me by the Spirit, I am living in supernatural gospel mode. I am living the gospel. And I find myself living better than I am able.

This is the gospel path. This is *life as it ought to be.*

A Glimpse of Glory — Cliff's Story

Cliff Boone was the first missionary supported by the church I helped begin in New Jersey. Cliff was a church-planting missionary to the Sandawe people group in Tanzania. The following is a story he told to his grandchildren about an experience he had while in Tanzania.

I stood on the shore of the island and looked out over Lake Victoria. It was early morning, and the sun was not yet hot. We had packed up all our things, and they were in a pile, along with many other people's luggage, in the sand by the water. A sailboat was just offshore. We were getting ready for our trip back to the mainland.

A week before, we had traveled all the way out to this little island named Ukara with Christians from the mainland. We had learned of this remote place from Timothy Mgasa, a stately old African man with gray hair, gray whiskers, and a distinguished British accent. He had learned English many years before when the British were in charge of the country. He was like a living history book, connecting us to the past with his stories. He and his family had become Christians in the great East African revival at a time when thousands upon thousands of people in East Africa gave their lives to Jesus Christ. Those days were over but he was alive to tell us about them. There was a light in Mr. Mgasa's eyes, joy in his heart, and a spring in his steps despite his advanced age.

He told us about the people on the island of Ukara who needed to hear the gospel, and about plans to send a choir to sing songs and preachers to preach the gospel to the islanders. He asked us if we wanted to go. Oh, we wanted to go! So we did.

Well, on that morning when I was standing on the beach, the meetings had ended and almost 100 people had believed in Jesus Christ as their Savior! It was a glorious time! They had asked me to be one of the preachers, and we enjoyed great days of sharing the gospel with those who hadn't believed while also visiting with precious African believers. There are so many stories I could tell (we even slept in a cleaned-out chicken coop with bats flying around our mosquito net!), but I want to tell you about our journey home.

As I stood on the beach, there was no land to be seen! It was like we were on a little mountaintop poking up from the clouds, and all around us, there was no other solid ground. Lake Victoria seems as big as the ocean.

We began picking up our things and putting them in the wooden sailboat, which was about as long as three Toyota Land Cruisers put end-to-end and about as wide as one of them. The mast which they had put in the center was a crooked trunk of a tree. Two other crooked poles cut from trees held the sail—one pole across the top and one at the bottom. The sail itself was sewn together from various pieces of cloth, with many rips and holes that had been patched, and more than a few that hadn't. Everything was a bit raggedy, but it was the only transportation we had.

We walked through the water and got into the boat when we realized that it was leaking. Water was coming up between the wooden slats at the bottom! So two men with little buckets began to scoop out the water as it came in, throwing it back into the lake.

Knowing that the leaking boat was the only way we were going to get home, we entrusted ourselves into the Lord's hands and climbed in. After everyone on the shore prayed for us and waved goodbye, they pushed the boat into deeper water. Wind filled the sail, and off we went!

After sailing for quite a long time, we could no longer see Ukara Island and we couldn't see the place where we were going, either. There was nothing but water. That's when it happened: the wind stopped.

We sat with the sail hanging limp. Not even a little breeze. No wind at all. The passengers had brought all sorts of things with them. Big fish that had been caught from the lake were being brought home to eat. One huge dead fish, as long as a bicycle, was underneath Bibi's [Swahili for grandmother] feet. Chickens whose legs had been tied together had been bundled up underneath some of the seats. With no wind to blow the smells away, our noses began to tell us just how stinky a boat with chickens and dead fish could be. On top of the luggage, and squeezed next to it and to the animals, were all the people: men and women all sitting in the blistering sun. It was high noon, so there was no shade, and there was no wind.

We sat there sweating in the sun for about an hour as the boat sat still in the water. At first, people talked, but after a while conversation stopped, and the only sound was of the two men with their buckets, scooping and throwing water out of the boat.

Mr. Mgasa and I were sitting together near the back, where the captain of the boat was also sitting. We were being treated as the special guests, he because of his age and character, and me because I was the foreign preacher. I turned to him and spoke very softly, "We need to pray and ask God for wind." I was thinking that we would pray silently, in our own hearts, but Mr. Mgasa looked at my face, thought for just a moment, and suddenly stood up.

"Everyone listen!" he called out. All the people turned and looked at him. Making a long, slow, sweeping motion with his arm until his open hand pointed to me, he said, "He is going to pray that God sends the wind!" Then he looked at me for another moment and sat down.

"Oh, my goodness," I thought to myself. "I wasn't expecting this! What if I pray and God doesn't answer?" I paused, and then God gave me courage. I slowly stood up, and as I did, every eye in the boat was looking at me. Even the two men with buckets stopped scooping. It was completely silent. I looked up into the cloudless sky and the blazing sun, glanced at the limp sail, and then I closed my eyes and raised my hands. With a loud voice, I worshipped God, and then, in Jesus' name, I said, "O God, send the wind!"

I sat back down. All the Christians said, "Amen." Everyone's eyes went from me to the sail. Would the wind come and fill it? Nothing happened. The sail hung lifeless and still.

The two men began to scoop the water again. No one spoke. I put my head down. And that's when I heard her; one of the ladies sitting near me whispered, "The sail! It's moving! Wind is coming!"

I looked up. The sail fluttered just a little bit. Then it fluttered a little longer. Then wind came and filled the sail and began to push the boat!

Mr. Mgasa shouted out, "Hallelujah! God has sent the wind!" All the Christians on the boat began to sing praises to God. Everyone smiled. The two men with buckets scooped faster.

A few hours later, as we came near to our landing place, the people on shore stopped what they were doing. "What is that noise?" they wondered. Then they realized that our boat was full of song. We sang all the way into our landing. Mr. Mgasa jumped off the boat and answered their questions. "Do you want to know why we are singing?" He told them the story of how God had sent the wind. They all listened to the story, and now you have heard the story, too!

CHAPTER SIX

Gospel Practices

~~

So we do not lose heart. Though our outer self is wasting away, our inner self is being renewed day by day. 2 Corinthians 4:16

Sometimes after preaching on a Sunday morning, I felt really good about my sermon. Perhaps people told me how helpful the sermon was, or perhaps I just felt that I "connected." I could live for several days on that feeling of success. But far too often, I left Sunday morning church with the dismaying feeling that I had failed. My wife's encouraging words seldom dispelled my gloom. My usual Monday morning response to this Sunday morning failure was to say, "I'll try harder this week!" It was the only response I knew to make, but it reflected my misunderstanding of the role of effort in the Christian experience as well as a misunderstanding of the gospel.

Grace and Works

While attending Bible college, I was taught that when a person becomes a Christian by grace through faith, there were four things he or she was supposed to do: read the Bible, pray, have fellowship with other Christians, and be a witness for Jesus. My impression at that time was that though becoming a Christian was by grace, living as a Christian was by works. As long as I did those four things, I was okay with God. And God was required to bless me.

It is not wrong to say that Christians are to read the Bible, pray, fellowship, and witness for Jesus. Those are all part of what I identify in this chapter as gospel practices: renewing the heart before God, building the gospel into one another, and engaging the world with the gospel.

So, what was my problem? I thought my efforts were a way to achieve the approval of God and others. The better I performed, the more approval I gained. I was stuck in performance mode. I failed to understand that effort in the Christian life flows out of grace. Good works are a result of grace. We engage in good works because we are already approved by God through Jesus, not to be approved. Though I understood that we become Christians through the gospel of grace, I seemed to think that we live the Christian life by works. I failed to understand that the entirety of the Christian experience is by grace through faith. We become believers by grace through faith and we live as Christians moment by moment by grace through faith. Good works in both conversion and the Christian experience are a response to grace, not a means of achieving grace. A key passage in this regard is Ephesians 2:8-10:

> [8]For by grace you have been saved through faith. [9]And this is not your own doing; it is the gift of God, not a result of works, so that no one may boast. [10]For we are his workmanship, created in Christ Jesus for good works, which God prepared beforehand, that we should walk in them.

What does it mean to be "saved"? Salvation includes both the beginning of the Christian experience and its everyday expression. Notice that verses 8 and 9 tell us that we are not saved by what we do but then verse 10 tells us that we are recreated in Christ "for" good works. We are not saved "by" good works, we are saved "for" good works. The effort of the Christian life is a response to the gospel of grace.

What then is the purpose of the gospel practices for the Christian? Why do we need to "do" the gospel? The practices *unleash* the power of the gospel *in us* and *through us.* They unleash the power of the gospel *in us* because the practices shape our souls, enabling us to live by faith moment by moment. And the practices unleash the power of the gospel *through us* as they empower our witness to the world. The practices are not ways to merit God's grace or favor but means of grace by which we experience the power of the gospel and demonstrate it. The practices are the experiential *means* of the *gospel way.*

Three Spheres of Life

The gospel practices are lived out in three life spheres: before God, with other believers, and in the world. Those three spheres are the areas of life in which each of us lives and are the domains in which we live out the three practices. We renew our hearts before *God,* we build the gospel into *one another's* lives, and we engage our *world* with the gospel in the power of the Spirit.

Three Daily Practices

The three gospel practices are daily practices. I have heard it said that the *problem* with the Christian life is that it is so daily. I prefer to say that the *power* of the Christian life is that it is so daily! The first of the three practices is heart renewal. We must daily renew our hearts before God. Paul says, "Though our outer self is wasting away, our inner self is being renewed *day by day*" (2 Corinthians 4:16). The second practice is daily building one another up in the gospel through New Testament community. Acts 2:46 tells us that the early church met "… *day by day*, attending the temple together and breaking bread in their homes…" The third daily practice is engaging our world in the task of mission. Acts 2:47 says, "And the Lord added to their number *day by day* those who were being saved." The Lord added people to the church day by day, but you can be sure that he used people to preach the gospel day by day. (Emphases added in the above verses.)

The only way to live fully as God intends is to live the three practices daily.

Three Word and Prayer Practices

Each of the practices is a "Word and prayer" practice.[25] We renew our hearts before God as we read or hear the Word of God and pray in response; we are built up in the gospel as we speak the Word of God to one another and as we pray together; and we engage our world through believing prayer and through speaking the Word of the gospel to our world.

Three Interdependent Practices

The three daily practices are interdependent and reciprocal. We must practice all three to fully enter human flourishing. We must live the gospel in all three spheres of life (before God, with one another, in the world) if we are to live well. They are like the legs of a three-legged stool; all three are necessary for the stool to function.

If we daily seek to renew our hearts but are not being built up through New Testament community and rarely or never seek to

---

[25] This insight came from my wife Patricia.

engage our world, then we are not living *life as it ought to be*. If we are deeply involved in gospel engagement but fail to take time for heart renewal, we are not living *life as it ought to be*. We need to live out all three daily gospel practices in order to live the way God intends.

The Three Practices

The three practices are renew, build, and engage.

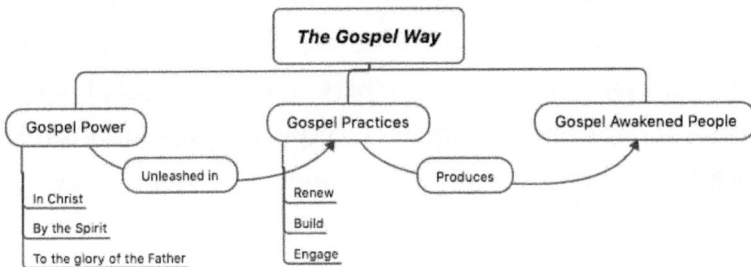

Let's consider each of the practices.

Practice One — The Renewing of the Heart Before God

The apostle Paul had a life-transforming and renewing experience on the road to Damascus when he encountered the resurrected Jesus.[26] While this dramatic experience was important, it was not sufficient for Paul to face the challenges that lay ahead. In 2 Corinthians 4:16, Paul says that though he was outwardly wasting away, in the inner person he was being "renewed day by day." Paul needed heart renewal each day.

---

[26] Acts 9.

One of my pastors[27] said in a recent sermon that he begins each day with "gospel amnesia." By this, he meant that he must remember to realign his heart, mind, and emotions with the gospel each day. This is true for all of us. The only way to experience moment by moment gospel power is through day by day renewal.

Aligning the heart

The purpose of day by day renewal is to align and realign our hearts with the gospel. We all align our hearts with something or someone or some desire. Often, we align our hearts with our own personal success or some cause or person. Every aspect of our living is a result of our heart alignment. To walk the *gospel way* is to align our hearts with the gospel of Jesus moment by moment, day by day, and more and more.

I grew up in Fort Lauderdale, Florida. The waves in the Atlantic Ocean at the Fort Lauderdale beach aren't usually very big but once in a while, they are big enough to body surf. Body surfing is surfing without a surfboard. To catch a wave, you must wait for the right wave and then wait for the right moment to throw your body into and with the wave just as it is beginning to break. If you catch the wave just right, you get a great ride all the way to the beach. The key is that you must align your body with the power of the wave, for the wave will not align its power with you!

Gospel alignment must be done with intentionality. We need to intentionally order our mind, will, and emotions around the gospel.

---

[27] Pastor John Franks of First Presbyterian Church in Augusta, Georgia. John says that he first heard that expression from another pastor.

As we intentionally align our hearts with God, we unleash the power of God into our living.

The pattern of renewal

There is a persistent pattern of spiritual renewal in the Scriptures; in particular, I see this pattern in Romans 12:1-2; Colossians 3:1-17; and Titus 2:11-14. Here is how I express the pattern.

Behold the glory. Renewal begins with God himself. In 2017, I began to see God's glory and wonder in a new way. In 2 Corinthians 3:18, Paul says, "And we all, with unveiled face, beholding the glory of the Lord, are being transformed into the same image from one degree of glory to another." As we increasingly behold God's glory in Christ, we cultivate a sense of awe and wonder that recreates our thinking, feeling, and doing.

Feel the weight (of sin and inadequacy). When we see the glory of God, the light of his glory begins to reveal the depth of our sin and inadequacy. Seeing the glory of God in 2017 caused me to see with new clarity the sinfulness of my heart and my insufficiency. I felt the weight of my sin.[28]

We read of Peter's encounter with Jesus and a great catch of fish in Luke 5, through which Peter caught a glimpse of who Jesus was. His response is recorded in Luke 5:8. "But when Simon Peter saw it, he fell down at Jesus' knees, saying, 'Depart from me, for I am a sinful man, O Lord.'" The right response to our sin and inadequacy

---

[28] The expression "feel the weight" is adapted from St. Anselm, who said that we need to consider the weight of sin. St. Anselm of Canterbury, *Cur Deus Homo: Why God Became a Man* (p. 70). Kindle Edition. "You have not as yet estimated the great burden of sin."

is repentance. Colossians 3:5-8 tells us to "put to death" the old way of thinking, feeling, and doing. We are to "put off the old self with its practices." We are not to manage our sin; we are to put it to death.

In particular, we must put to death the sin of pride, the sin of self-consciousness,[29] and self-promotion. Nothing will quench[30] the power of the Spirit like pride.

Embrace the wonder (of Christ in us, by the Spirit, for the Father's glory). This awareness of sin and inadequacy leads us to embrace the gospel. In 2017, I caught a glimpse of God's glory and became aware of the depth of my sin. This set me free to embrace the joy of the gospel, to embrace the wonder of my union with Jesus by the Spirit. I embrace the wonder of the gospel when I am *aware* of Christ in me, *expect* the Spirit's power, and *pursue* the Father's glory.

Renewing the heart at the beginning of the day

We must renew our hearts to begin our day. In Psalm 90:14, the psalmist prays, "Satisfy us in the morning with your steadfast love…" How we begin the day is important. If we begin focusing on the bad news of our world (via our news feeds), the bad news of venting, angst, and anger (through social media—or so I have heard), or just the ordinary challenges of the day ("How will I pay that bill this month?"), it will deeply affect how we live our day. So, I seek to begin my day by aligning my heart with the truth of the gospel.

---

[29] I define self-consciousness as an undue awareness of oneself and an over-concern with what others think of us.

[30] 1 Thessalonians 5:19.

"The first great and primary business to which I ought to attend every day is to have my soul happy in the Lord." [31] — *George Mueller*

Gospel skill: The Sword of the Spirit Devotional Journey.

Each day, at the beginning of the day, I take time to read the Bible and pray through an approach to prayer and Bible reading that I call the *Sword of the Spirit Devotional Journey.*[32] This is not just a Bible reading plan, but a devotional journey. The purpose of the *Sword of the Spirit Devotional Journey* is not just Bible knowledge, but a renewed heart, a heart set aflame by the word of God and the Spirit of God. The purpose is not just information but transformation. We read the Bible to behold the glory of God, to feel the weight of our sin and inadequacy, and to embrace the gospel. Although I recommend using the *M'Cheyne's Bible Reading Guide,*[33] the *Sword of the Spirit Devotional Journey* can be used with almost any reading plan. It is not just about *what* we read, but about *how* we read.

The heart of the *Sword of the Spirit Devotional Journey* is that it seeks to be both comprehensive and contemplative. We need to read through the Bible in a comprehensive way so that over time we read and begin to grasp the whole counsel of God. But we also must think deeply about smaller portions of Scripture so that our hearts are renewed and transformed. Psalm 1 tells us that it is the person

---

[31] George Mueller, "The First Great and Primary Business," Georgemueller.org, 7/3/2017, https://www.georgemuller.org/devotional/the-first-great-and-primary-business.

[32] For more information on the *SOS Journey,* see the appendix.

[33] *M'Cheynes Bible Reading Guide* as adapted by Don Carson. http://www.edginet.org/mcheyne/year_carson_a4.pdf.

who delights in the words of God and who meditates day and night on God's words who is like a flourishing tree. Contemplation or meditation allows the Scripture to take root in the heart. To accomplish these two purposes (comprehensive reading and contemplative reading) on the *Journey,* we read carefully, we ponder deeply, we pray fervently, and we live and share faithfully.

We read carefully — We read the Bible both extensively and intensively. We read a longer portion (reading extensively). For most this would be two chapters each day. As we read, we seek to discern what smaller portion of our reading the Spirit would have us ponder more deeply (reading intensively) for that day. This smaller portion could be a verse or verses, a portion of a chapter, or sometimes a whole chapter.

We ponder deeply — We read the verse or verses slowly, observantly, seeking to discern meaning and apply the passage to our lives. We ask three questions: "What does it say?" "What does it mean?" and "What does it say to me today?"

We pray fervently — We cannot fully live the passage until we have prayed the passage! We pray from the smaller portion of Scripture for that day, praising God for what the passage tells us about his worth and asking God for our need which is exposed in the passage and for other needs.

We live and share faithfully — We then take that smaller portion of Scripture into our daily lives. As best we can, seeking to walk by the Spirit, we integrate the truth we learned into our daily living. And it is important to seek to share what the Spirit taught us through the Word with someone else each day.[34] Sharing what we learned with someone else is good for them and good for us. We learn best when we teach others.

I know this short description of the *Sword of the Spirit Journey* is insufficient, so I have included more detailed information on how to walk this devotional journey in the appendix.

Renewing the heart throughout the day

But it is not enough to align our hearts with the gospel to begin our day; we must live with a renewed awareness of the presence of Jesus by the Spirit throughout our day. How do we do this? We must live present tense, practicing the presence of God in this one moment. This means to practice the presence of Christ, live in the power of the Spirit, and to the Father's agenda as fully as possible in this one moment.

Realigning the heart

Inevitably, throughout the day, my affections (mind, will, and emotions) stray from the *gospel way* I am seeking to walk. What do I do? I must realign my heart with the gospel. The Bible gives us a simple two-part rhythm as a means of doing this: repentance and faith. Repentance is confession and turning, acknowledging my wrong and going a different way. Repentance is both before God and before people. Martin Luther famously wrote that "repentance is all of life." Faith is aligning our hearts again with the gospel, remembering that I am united with Jesus, that I am to walk by the Spirit, and that I am always to seek the Father's better agenda.

---

[34] I learned the idea of sharing what we learn with others from my friends Lou Prontnicki and Dennis Spinney. Each credits the other, so I am crediting both!

When I drive down the road, I constantly make small corrections, realigning my car with the road. In this way, I avoid the ditches on the side of the road. When we live the gospel, we must constantly make small corrections (repentance and faith) to realign our affections with the Triune God. When my heart begins to stray, I immediately bring it back to center through repentance and faith.

I am sometimes discouraged by the need to repent often for the same sins. Just days ago, I learned this lesson from a friend: "Ongoing repentance is progress."[35] Through repentance and faith we realign our hearts.

Renewing the heart at the end of the day

It is also helpful to end each day by giving some thought to where we experienced the power and presence of God and where we failed to experience the power and presence of God during that day. According to how tired I am, this may take a few moments or a few minutes. I confess my sin and failure, give thanks to God for his presence, and drift off to sleep. However we do this, we must renew our hearts to begin our day, renew our hearts as we live our day, and then seek to renew our hearts at the end of the day.

An intentional plan

Your approach to gospel renewal will be different from mine. However you do it, it is important that you be intentional about renewing your heart in the gospel each day. Ask God to help you develop an approach that works for you.

---

[35] Thanks to Pastor Rick Ravis for this helpful idea.

Practice Two — Building One Another Up in the Gospel

This is the second daily practice. We build one another up in the gospel. The apostle Paul often used the metaphor of building to describe the purpose of community (emphasis in bold below is added):

- "So then let us pursue what makes for peace and for **mutual upbuilding**" (Romans 14:19).

- "Let each of us please his neighbor for his good, **to build him up**" (Romans 15:2).

- "For even if I boast a little too much of our authority, which the Lord gave for **building you up** and not for destroying you, I will not be ashamed" (2 Corinthians 10:8).

- "Have you been thinking all along that we have been defending ourselves to you? It is in the sight of God that we have been speaking in Christ, and all for your **upbuilding**, beloved" (2 Corinthians 12:19).

- "For this reason I write these things while I am away from you, that when I come I may not have to be severe in my use of the authority that the Lord has given me for **building up** and not for tearing down" (2 Corinthians 13:10).

We cannot live the Christian life in isolation. Christianity is a participatory endeavor. We must live the community that is described in Scripture, intentionally building one another up in the gospel. This has structural implications. We gather as a larger community on Sunday mornings, but as one of my pastors recently said, "Sunday worship is essential but not enough."[36] To live the Christian life the way God intends, we must also gather in smaller communities so that we can build one another up through the *"one another"* Bible verses of the New Testament. We are to love one another, bear with one another, be patient with one another, build one another up, etc. Some have counted as many as 59 *"one anothers"* in the New Testament. Living out these *"one anothers"* is how we move beyond the superficial to experience the supernatural, but many aren't practiced easily in large groups.

Cal Newport tells us that smaller groups work better than larger groups. Speaking of a business context, he says, "Though there's no specific team size that consistently emerges as optimal, essentially every result falls into a narrow range of roughly four to twelve people…"[37]

The biblical pattern is that we gather as a large community but also as smaller communities. In Acts 2:47, the church gathered both as a large community (thousands) and in smaller communities (housefuls). The early church often met in homes, thus limiting the number of people in any one gathering. Wayne Meeks tells us the smaller community is the "basic cell of the Christian movement."[38] Smaller communities are the basic building blocks of the church.

---

[36] Pastor Mike Phillips.

[37] Cal Newport, *A World Without Email: Reimagining Work in an Age of Communication Overload* (New York: Penguin Publishing Group. Kindle edition), 87.

[38] Wayne A. Meeks, *The First Urban Christians: the Social World of the Apostle Paul*, 2nd Edition (New Haven: Yale University Press, 2003), 75.

New Testament community

In September 2020, a year prior to finishing my ministry at Christ Community Church, I asked the church leaders to read the New Testament together, searching for what the Bible had to say about community. Each of the six of us read a portion of the New Testament and then we came together to report on what we learned. Here is a partial summary of what we discovered:

- The emphasis on love is consistent (John 14-16).
- We are not to speak evil of one another (James 4:11).
- We are to confess sins to one another (James 5:9).
- Believers are not to show partiality (James 2).
- We are called to love one another earnestly from a pure heart (1 Peter 1:22).
- We are to be a community where the excellencies of Jesus flow forth (1 Peter 2.9).
- We need to live with one another in humility and be willing to lay down our lives for one another (1 John 2:16).
- We are to build one another up in the holy faith (Jude 20).
- The church is in a spiritual battle (the Book of Revelation).
- We are to love one another as Christ has loved us (John 13:34-35).
- We are to bear much fruit that remains (John 15:16).

This, I realized, was the community my heart yearned for. This was the kind of community that I needed if I was to live consistently in Christ, by the Spirit, and to the glory of the Father. This was the kind of community I needed if I was to live a life of ongoing awakening. But it seemed clear to me that the community I most often experienced fell far short of what the New Testament described.[39]

Four aspects of New Testament community

From my study, I discerned four primary aspects of New Testament community.

1) *Speaking the gospel into one another community* — We are to speak the Word of God into one another's life circumstances. We speak the gospel to one another to build each other up. (Jude 20, "But you, beloved, building yourselves up in your most holy faith and praying in the Holy Spirit...") Thus we are not passive in New Testament community but actively speak the gospel to one another, instruct one another, and even rebuke one another.

2) *Life together community* — We do life together in openness, honesty, and brokenness. There is no substitute for spending time with one another. We do life together (Acts 2:42-44, "And they devoted themselves to the apostles' teaching and the fellowship, to the breaking of bread and the prayers..."). This community includes eating together, laughing together, and spending time together.

To be the people of God we must live in openness and honesty with one another. Norman Grubb tells us that we need to be "two-

---

[39] This is intended as a criticism of no one but me. Most often I was the one who led the smaller communities in which I participated.

way people."[40] That is, we are to be open and honest before God and open and honest before one another. He talks about the walls of respectability and self-esteem that keep us from healthy honesty and the need to tear down those walls.[41] When I have talked to other pastors about this idea of honesty and brokenness before one another, the comment I sometimes received is something like, "Well, you have to be careful about that…" They raise the concern of inappropriate confession and honesty. Yes, there can be inappropriate honesty, but there is also an openness and honesty that is appropriate and necessary for spiritual health. The best context for this kind of honesty is most often smaller communities within the larger community of the church.

At a recent men's Bible study, the passage we were looking at spoke of pride and the need for humility. The leader of the study asked, "Who is the prophet talking about?" I think he wanted us to say, "Judah, the southern kingdom of Israel," but instead I said, "I think he is talking about me." From there, I went on to confess before my brothers my self-consciousness and pride and tendency to compare myself with others. I tore down, at least a little, my wall of pride and respectability. We must have this kind of appropriate openness if we are to live as the people of God.

3) ***Praying together community*** — We pray together fervently and regularly. In Acts 4 the first church was under pressure; they responded by praying together: "And when they heard it, they lifted their voices together to God and said, 'Sovereign Lord, who made the heaven and the earth and

---

[40] Norman Grubb, *Continuous Revival: The Secret of Victorious Living* (Fort Washington, PA: CLC Publications, 1952), 18.
[41] Grubb, Continuous Revival, 21.

the sea and everything in them…'" The first church was power-filled because they regularly and fervently prayed together.

4) ***Engaging the world with the gospel community*** — We encourage one another to engage the world with the gospel (Acts 2:46, "And the Lord added to their number day by day those who were being saved."). We need to stir one another up to love and good works (Hebrews 10:24). These good works include engaging our world with the gospel of Jesus. Recently, I heard Pastor Mike Rasmussen say this: "Every community where Jesus is present is missional because he is missional."[42]

Gospel skill: living as part of a micro-community

I call small communities that seek to live out these four aspects of community *micro-communities.*[43] The four aspects of New Testament community cannot be well lived in large groups alone; we must form smaller communities within the larger community in order to live out the *"one anothers"* of the gospel. Timothy Gombis says that the church should be "communities of God's resurrection-powered presence."[44] But to fully experience this "resurrection-powered presence," we must walk together in the deep community that can only happen in smaller communities of faith.

---

[42] Mike Rasmussen, sermon at First Presbyterian Church, Augusta, GA, July 23, 2023.

[43] I got the name "micro-community" from Pastor Mike Hearon, lead pastor at First Presbyterian Church in Augusta, GA.

[44] Timothy G. Gombis, *Power in Weakness: Paul's Transformed Vision for Ministry* (Grand Rapids: William B. Eerdmans Publishing Company, 2021), 8.

Micro-communities are discipling communities. The micro-community, I believe, is the primary context of deep discipleship. It is in the micro-community that we learn to live the *gospel way.* The micro-community is the nexus of the *gospel way.* The word 'nexus' means that which connects or is the center of something. The micro-community is the nexus where all the aspects of living the gospel come together. The micro-community is the practical center of the *gospel way.* It is in the micro-community that we learn to live *in Christ, by the Spirit, for the glory of the Father.* It is in the micro-community that the daily practices of the gospel are learned and experienced. It is in the micro-community where we become the people God intends us to be.

Micro-communities are daily communities. Living as part of a micro-community is a daily part of life. Micro-communities will not usually meet daily in a formal sense[45] (we all have busy schedules and busy lives), but each day, we find a way to encourage, exhort, and build one another up in the gospel. Hebrews 3:13 tells us to "…exhort one another every day…" We may build others up through a phone call, a text, an email, a handwritten note, or a quick visit to see how someone is doing. However we do it, it is only within the context of a deep New Testament-type community that is something like a micro-community that the supernatural flourishing of the gospel happens.

Micro-communities are risky communities. Why do we often fail to live in such community? It is because we rightly see that such open, honest community is risky. Things may not go well.

---

[45] As my friend Carl Martin has pointed out to me, the daily gathering recorded in Acts 2 may have been a bit extraordinary. People had to get back to the ordinary tasks of life, the sheep needed care, the fields required tending, etc.

Relationships can be messy. This kind of community is inconvenient. But followers of Jesus must take the risk, for New Testament community is essential for *life as it ought to be*.

We build each other up in the gospel as we do life together in micro-communities. The church cannot be the light in the world that God intends without deep New Testament community, which leads into the third renewing practice.

Practice Three — Engaging Our World with the Gospel

Renewing the heart and building one another up in the gospel lead to the third daily practice: engaging our world with the gospel in the power of the Holy Spirit. Engaging the world must be the overflow of a life that daily seeks renewal of the heart and daily seeks to build up other believers and be built up by other believers. Renewing, building, and engaging are organically related. Engaging the world is about demonstrating the gospel and proclaiming the gospel.

Demonstrating the gospel

Demonstrating the gospel by how we live (good works) is the context of our engagement with the world. Gary Tyra says, "We are seeking to shape a community of faith that can image, even if imperfectly, the reality and nature of the kingdom."[46] It is out of that gospel-shaped community that the gospel overflows into our world. Thus, we must demonstrate *life as it ought to be*. The world needs to be amazed at the reality of Christ in us by the Spirit.

---

[46] Tyra, *Introduction to Spirituality*, 89.

Proclaiming the gospel

We demonstrate the gospel so we can proclaim the gospel. To engage our world, we must proclaim the wonder of participation in Christ and his resurrection. It is never enough to live the gospel; we must proclaim the gospel. We see this in 1 Peter 2:9, "But you are a chosen race, a royal priesthood, a holy nation, a people for his own possession, that you may proclaim the excellencies of him who called you out of darkness into his marvelous light." We enter into our purpose when we proclaim the excellencies of our God to one another but also to our world.

A daily practice

Gospel engagement is not to be a once-in-a-while activity. It is a daily practice. This does not mean that we will find opportunities to speak the gospel every day, but it does mean that we daily pray for specific people and for gospel opportunity, that we daily seek to develop new relationships, and that we daily expect and seek opportunities and are prepared to speak the gospel.

A few weeks ago, I was in the hot tub at my gym after swimming laps. A young man who worked for the gym sat nearby. I engaged him in conversation. I learned he is home-schooled and works part-time for the gym. It turned out that I knew one of his friends. I asked him if he attended church. He said he did but wasn't very involved. I briefly shared my life-changing experience of the gospel. We ended our conversation because he had some duties to attend to, but minutes later, before I got out of the hot tub, he came back and said, "Tell me more about what happened to you!" We discover our purpose when we engage our world with the gospel.

An overflowing practice

As we live the *gospel way*, over time the result is that we are more and more "filled with all the fullness of God."[47] This is essential to gospel engagement. Imagine I have a large pitcher of water. I begin to pour that large container of water into a small glass. As I pour, the water begins to fill the glass until it is wholly filled. If I continue to pour water into the glass it will overflow. Overflow is essential to the work of gospel engagement. As we renew our hearts daily and as we daily build the gospel into one another, we are more and more filled with the fullness of God. As we continue to live the *gospel way*, the gospel begins to overflow into our living and speaking. Engaging our world apart from the renewing of the heart and New Testament community will lack the fullness of gospel power.

A Spirit-empowered practice

Acts 1:8 tells us, "But you will receive power when the Holy Spirit comes on you, and you will be my witnesses in Jerusalem, and in all Judea and Samaria, and to the ends of the earth." We can only engage the world well by the power of the Spirit. We cannot successfully engage our world with the gospel in our own strength; but in the power of the Spirit, we can. We are only ready to step into the clash of cultures if we have first stepped into the presence of God in Christ, by the power of the Spirit, and for the purpose of God. The Spirit is given so that we might engage our world with the gospel. If we are not engaging our world with the gospel, we are not living a Spirit-empowered life!

---

[47] Ephesians 3:19.

A strategic practice

For me, evangelism (which means to communicate the gospel, the good news) too often felt like a duty to be done. I did it (after all, as a pastor, I was supposed to speak the gospel), but it never felt like the overflow of Christ in me. But as I have learned to live the gospel in Christ and by the Spirit, evangelism has more and more become the overflow of the gospel at work in me. Now, when I speak the gospel to others, it is Christ *in* me and the community of faith speaking *through* me. Evangelism is not first a strategy, but a life lived.

Yet, we need strategies. Here is a primary way I have learned to speak the gospel to my world:

Gospel skill: B.L.E.S.S.

I first heard of the acronym B.L.E.S.S. from Dennis Henderson, a leader of the *6:4 Fellowship*, but later I discovered that there is a book by that same name.[48] The acronym B.L.E.S.S. stands for:

Begin with prayer — Pray daily for specific people and for opportunities to engage your world. I have learned to create a "Gospel List" for my daily prayer. This is a list of friends, neighbors, coworkers, and others to whom I am seeking to speak the gospel. A "Gospel List" then, is a list of people for whom I am daily praying to come to faith in Jesus.

Listen — Care enough to listen to other people's stories. Cultivate the habit of listening well. Listening well means asking questions. The right questions are respectful of the person you are

---

[48] Dave Ferguson and Jon Ferguson, *B.L.E.S.S.: 5 Everyday Ways to Love Your Neighbor and Change the World* (Washington D.C.: Salem Books, 2021).

talking to and lead the conversation to go beyond the superficial toward the big questions of the gospel. I learned from Mike Hearon, my pastor and friend, to ask, *"Where are you on your spiritual journey?"* I have discovered that most people gladly tell me something about their spiritual journey. And if I listen well, I often have opportunity to share something about my story and *the* story.

Eat — Eat together with those you are getting to know. Eating together is about more than food; it is about relationship. Invite others into your life by eating with them.

Serve — Look for opportunities to serve others.

Share — Share your story and share *the* story—the gospel story.

When I first heard this approach, I thought "I can do this!" And then I thought, "Anyone can do this!" We can pray daily, we can learn to care and listen, we can invite others into our lives, we can look for opportunities to serve... and as we do so there will be opportunities to share our story. I have stopped putting myself under the pressure of having a duty to share the gospel. Instead, I have started to begin each day praying for specific people and for opportunities to engage people. I seek to be interested in people. I learn their names, listen to their stories, and invite them into my life as I can. I seek to develop new relationships. I serve them when I can. And then I share as I have opportunity.

I was so struck by this simple relational approach to evangelism that in my last year as pastor at Christ Community Church, my wife and I offered to personally buy a copy of the book *B.L.E.S.S.* for anyone in the church who asked for one. It was good for us that we were not a large church at that time, for just about everyone requested one!

Here is one story that pictures what gospel engagement can look like: I was flying to New York City to visit a friend in the spring of 2021. Before I left, I prayed for opportunities to speak the gospel during the trip. On the flight from Augusta, Georgia to LaGuardia Airport in New York City. I sat next to a young man returning from the *Masters* golf tournament. I asked him about himself and his work, etc., and learned a lot about him. I really listened. After a while, I asked, "Let me ask you a different sort of question. Where are you on your spiritual journey?" He responded, "You are going to have to unpack that!" And for the remainder of the flight that is what we did; we talked about the good news of Jesus. At the end of the flight, he said to me, "I have never talked with anyone for an entire flight before!"

On the flight back from New York, I sat next to a Muslim young lady. After learning much about her, I asked, "Where are you on your spiritual journey?" That led to a conversation that took most of the flight. She was so interested that she took notes!

Engaging our world with the gospel is the fruit of daily renewal of the heart and seeking to daily build the gospel into one another. It is the fruit of seeking to live *in Christ, by the Spirit, for the glory of the Father.*

Three Reviving Practices

The three practices (renew, build, engage) are God-given means by which God's power is unleashed in us and through us. These three practices are the 'places' where our experience of God's power is nurtured and where God's power is unleashed into our world. They are God's means of revival.

The great need of our day is revival: revival first of our hearts as individuals and then revival of our churches. Through these practices, we "set our sails to catch the wind from heaven."[49] The three practices do not *cause* revival to happen, but as we live these daily practices, we set the sails of our souls to capture the reviving wind of the Holy Spirit! Renew — Build — Engage — set your sails…

[49] G. Campbell Morgan, quoted in John Kilpatrick, Larry Sparks, and Michael L. Brown, *The Fire that Never Sleeps: Keys for Sustaining Personal Revival* (Shippensburg: Destiny Image Publishers, INC., 2015), 227.

A Glimpse of Glory — Jason's Story

I am not special. Not a prophet or an apostle. But I am a follower of Jesus. I am a follower of Jesus who has heard the voice of Jesus!

In 2014/2015, I was preparing to marry my now-wife, Anna. I had a Bible degree. I was working on my Master's in Christian Ministry. I was serving as a youth and young adult pastor in a local church. I was busy.

Over four months, I would leave my seemingly secure job as a youth pastor, get married, find out that we were expecting our first child, and begin to work on planting a church...in that order.

As my time at the local church was coming to an end, one Friday night, Anna and I had invited a few friends to her apartment for dinner. Both of us looked forward to this, as we greatly needed the encouragement of these friends. The days were so often overwhelmed by wedding planning and stress over the future, so she and I both looked for time to escape with those we loved.

I journeyed to her apartment that evening, all the while beginning to feel sick. I could feel my face getting more and more heated, and sure enough, I had managed to come down with something radically quick and totally overwhelming. By the time I reached her apartment, I was running a 100-degree-plus fever and was noticeably feeling ill.

This was a pre-COVID world. In that world, we simply decided to carry on——as people used to do before q-tipped noses and quarantined Thanksgivings. But I was so ill that I could not bring myself to participate in the evening's plans. Anna and I decided that I would lie down in her bedroom while she entertained; I'd be there if she needed me and then leave for home after "the boys" left.

Again, she took my temperature, which was over 100 degrees. I crawled to her room, lay down, and wept. All of the stress of this moment flooded my heart. I began (as many of us do at times) to complain to God:

"How have you gotten me into this mess?"

"I try so hard to live the life you called me to. I try so hard…"

After silence, I added, "I'm leaving my ministry. I'm getting married. And now, on top of it all, I'm sick. I can't even enjoy a meal with my friends."

The room remained silent and shaded in lines of leaves flooding through cracked windows, cascaded by the sun to the walls.

At some point, I fell asleep while intermittently praying, "Lord, please heal me of whatever this is." I'd open my eyes as the sun slowly dimmed, only to close them again. "Lord, whatever this is, would you please take it from me?" It was at that moment that an indescribable feeling overtook me. In an instant, as the leaves continued to rustle outside, their shadows stopped moving along the gray industrial lines of the cracker box walls of Anna's room. There was a great sense of something changing, and I felt better, but still, there was silence.

I was awake. Sweat dripping from me, lungs heaving…but awake. At that precise moment, I heard clearly something I will never ever forget for the rest of my life.

"Jason. Even this, I am in control of. Even this."

I know that it is passé for people to claim to have heard the voice of God. I know some will read this and roll their eyes. I know many will simply chalk this one up to exaggeration, linguistic ability, or craft. I want it to be said that if this story is not true, everything the Lord has done in my life should be chalked up to the same.

I am not saying that I heard his voice in some metaphorical way in my head. What I am saying is that God spoke clearly to me that day. I sat in that bed, awake and uncontrollably crying. I could barely utter my response as I asked, "Are you Jesus the Nazarene?" To which I again heard, "Jason. Even this, I am in control of. Even this." It was then that I felt at peace.

I lay there wishing that moment would never end. I could not imagine my life without it. Yet, in time, whatever had happened was just that: something that had happened. The room again went silent, the leaves in shadow swept across my tear-filled face, and I felt better. My fever was gone. My body ache was gone. My sore throat was gone. I was well.

I immediately called my father and, through choking tears, tried to tell him what had just happened to me. He (of course) thought that something horrible had happened. His 29-year-old son was calling him hysterical. I eventually calmed him down as I calmed myself down. I told him the story, and we both sat in silence on the phone. I could hear him as he sought to contemplate the reality of it all—as, like me, he had started to cry. "That was Jesus," he said. "Jason, that was Jesus." We hung up the phone, and I entered the room where Anna and our friends were sharing their meal.

They sat in the living room, staring at me as I stared at them. They must have wondered if, in some strange fever dream, I was lost and wandering. I asked Anna if she would take my temperature. She did. It was normal. I was fine.

Here is the astounding thing: I went from being sicker than I can ever remember to being completely well. My friends had seen me desperately sick only minutes earlier, and now I was completely well. It was clear to me that the Lord was showing me something: something that was profound. Here is what I learned: no matter my life situation, he is in control. Not me. And God is gracious and kind.

Indeed, the difficulties of my life at that time did continue. Leaving my former ministry was difficult. I experienced animosity, and my character was assaulted. Financially, this created hardship in our new marriage. Anna and I began our married life together with many spiritual battles.

As the months went by, I was sometimes dejected and disappointed by the loss of another possible ministry position. I was saddened as another ship set sail, only to disappear into the murky depths of a lost hope. It was in those moments that again I would hear, "Jason. Even this, I am in control of. Even this."

Jason Filbert, church planter with the Bible Fellowship Church, Naples, Florida

CHAPTER SEVEN

Gospel Awakened People

~

> *But the fruit of the Spirit is love, joy, peace, patience, kindness, goodness, faithfulness, gentleness, self-control; against such things there is no law. Galatians 5:22-23*

In November 2021, my younger sister Cathy (who should know such things) said, "You are a different person." She didn't mean that everything about me was different. I am still a bit introspective (okay, more than a bit), can still be moody, have the same strange sense of humor (though I laugh more now), and still love to read. I think she meant that she sees a new joy, a new love, and a new boldness in my living. What she sees, I believe, is the fruit of living *life as it ought to be.* She sees someone who has been awakened to the power of the gospel.

Gospel Awakening

As you now know, *life as it ought to be* is simply one way of expressing what it means to live the gospel. As we consistently live the moment by moment aspects of the *gospel way* (in Christ, by the Spirit, to the glory of the Father), the power of the gospel is unleashed through the daily gospel practices (renew, build, and engage) in us and through us. This more and more awakens us to the wonder and beauty of God in Christ. Gospel awakening should be the normal experience of the believer.

Conformed to the Image of Jesus

As we live this gospel-awakened life, we become more and more like Jesus—we increasingly resemble the new creations in Christ that the apostle Paul says we already are. "If anyone is in Christ, he is a new creation. The old has passed away; behold, the new has come" (2 Corinthians 5:17). *Life as it ought to be* is about the awakening of the soul to the wonder and beauty of Christ in us but also the forming of the soul into the image of Jesus. As we live the *gospel way*, the character of Jesus is formed in us. In Romans 8:29, Paul tells us, "For those whom he foreknew he also predestined to be conformed to the image of his Son..."

As the character of Jesus is formed in us, we begin to respond differently to life's challenges even when we are not consciously thinking of living in Christ by the Spirit. Back when I would bike on the roads of New Jersey with friends, my bike had "clipless" pedals with special shoes that "clip" into and unclip from the pedals.[50] Unclipping your feet from the pedals requires that you twist your ankle in a certain way. Once, in the beginning, I was stopped with my right foot out of the pedals and the left clipped in. I leaned a bit to the left, and the only way to keep from falling was to unclip my left foot—but I didn't have time to remember how to do it. There was nothing I could do, and over I went. But over time, I developed what is called "muscle memory." I could clip and unclip my feet without thinking about what I needed to do.

Christian character is like that. As the character of Jesus is formed in us, over time, we begin to talk differently and respond to

---

[50] Thus, "clipless" is a misnomer.

life's challenges differently, even when we aren't consciously thinking about such things. We develop "soul memory."

More and More

This Spirit-produced soul formation is progressive. We can live *in Christ* at any moment, but becoming like Jesus is a lifetime's work. It is a progressive transformation. Paul speaks of this progress in several places (emphasis in bold added):

- "And this is my prayer: that your love may abound **more and more** in knowledge and depth of insight…" (Philippians 1:9).

- "May the Lord make your love **increase and overflow** for each other and for everyone else, just as ours does for you" (1 Thessalonians 3:12).

- "As for other matters, brothers and sisters, we instructed you how to live in order to please God, as in fact you are living. Now we ask you and urge you in the Lord Jesus to do this **more and more**" (1 Thessalonians 4:1).

- "And in fact, you do love all of God's family throughout Macedonia. Yet we urge you, brothers and sisters, to do so **more and more**…" (1 Thessalonians 4:10).

Three Gospel Fruits

As we live the gospel-awakened life, three gospel fruits begin to overflow into our lives: a new joy, a new love, and a new boldness.

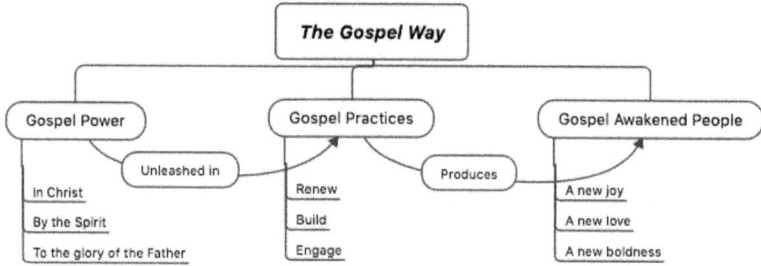

The First Fruit — A New Joy

The first mark of a spiritually awakened person is a new joy. The response of the first Christians in the Book of Acts can only be characterized as a response of joy. They lived in a time of brokenness, but Christ had come, and the Spirit had been given. How could they not be joyful?

What is joy? Joy is an emotion but more than an emotion. It is a deep sense of well-being. It is a sense of well-being "...*over* something... that we perceive as very good."[51] Joy, then, is a sense of well-being that is *because* of something.

Temporary joy

There can be a joy that comes about because of some natural circumstance.[52] When the girl says "Yes!" to the young man's marriage proposal, he feels joyful. He perceives her acceptance of his offer as very good—as he should. And yet, it is, in the end, a temporary joy. It is temporary because all the joys of this world are

---

[51] Daniel J. Denk, *An Introduction to Joy: the Divine Journey to Human Flourishing* (Grand Rapids: William B. Eerdmans Publishing, 2023), 4.

[52] My youngest daughter Sarah helped me to see this more clearly.

temporary. All temporary joys are ultimately intended to be replaced by a far greater joy.

These natural joys are not to be disparaged because they are temporary, for they are good gifts of God. But as good gifts of God, they point to a greater joy. Therefore, there can be genuine joy over some events or circumstances in this world, but it is always a temporary joy because this is a temporary, passing-away world. If all we have are temporary joys, in the end, we will be joyless.

Transcendent joy[53]

But Christians are called to live with a joy that does not pass away. Christians are called to live with joy no matter our circumstances. Joy is a sense of well-being experienced in good times and in times of affliction and difficulty.[54] Therefore, joy is more than an emotion (though it involves our emotions). It is a settled attitude of the heart.

We are told to "Rejoice always"—that is, in all circumstances (1 Thessalonians 5:16). This requires that our joy be based on something or someone who transcends the circumstances of this world. We are called to always rejoice, be glad, exult, and delight. We are called to a transcendent joy. But how is this possible in this broken and too often joyless world?

A transcendent joy is possible because it is *anticipatory*. The bride awaiting her wedding day has the joy of anticipation. Some irritation may intrude on her day, but she looks past it to the joy of the wedding ceremony. Such is the joy of the Christian. Psalm 30:5

---

[53] I first heard the term "transcendent joy" from my friend David Blair.
[54] James 1:2 says, "Count it all joy, my brothers, when you meet trials of various kinds…"

tells us, "Weeping may tarry for the night, but joy comes with the morning." In Hebrews 12:2, we are told to "[look] to Jesus, the founder and perfecter of our faith, who for the joy that was set before him endured the cross…" Like Jesus, we look ahead to the joy set before us. As Pastor Mike Hearon has said, "The best thing about you [the Christian] is your future."

But our joy is not only anticipatory but also *present-tense* joy. For the Christian, eternity has invaded the present. God is always present in Christ and by the Spirit. He is with us, in us, and for us. Psalm 16:11 tells us, "In your presence there is fullness of joy…" We are told in Philippians 4:4 to rejoice, not in our circumstances, but "in the Lord," who is always present with us. A transcendent joy is possible because the Spirit who dwells in us produces "love, joy…" (Galatians 5:22). Paul tells us that the essence of the Christian life is a life of joy: "For the kingdom of God is not a matter of eating and drinking but of righteousness and peace and joy in the Holy Spirit" (Romans 14:17).

The first thing I noticed when I experienced spiritual renewal in 2017 was a new joy: a joy that hadn't been there before but then suddenly was. Nothing in my circumstances had changed, and yet there was joy. Here is an excerpt from an article I wrote for our denominational magazine, *One Voice*:

> I began, from Scripture, crying out to God in prayers of worship and adoration. As I did, I became aware of my fallenness. He opened my eyes. God opened my eyes to the depths of my rebellion and self-focus. I began to confess and repent of sin. As I did, something unusual (for me) happened: an emotion flooded my heart. I asked myself, "What is that feeling, that emotion?" Then I thought, "That must be joy!" Joy flooded my

heart. But it wasn't joy for a moment, or joy for a day, or even for a few days; it has been a joy that has continued for the last two years. I don't always *feel* joyful, but I seek to always "rejoice" (Philippians 4:4). I believe I can honestly say that I am now a joyful person.[55]

How can we have joy in a world that so often seems joyless? We can have joy because, ultimately, it is not our joy—it is his joy. When we live the *gospel way*, we step into the joy of the Father, the Son, and the Holy Spirit. As Charles Mathewes describes it, "Ecstatic, joyful praise is humanity's end and current glory."[56] My friend Mike Phillips says we are called not only to experience joy in the end (that will be a joy-filled day) but to discover joy on the journey.

Joy and enjoyment

This joy is what enables us to *enjoy* life. I didn't know how to enjoy life most of my life. I didn't know how to laugh, and I didn't know how to enjoy the good things God brought into my life. I wanted to enjoy life, I just didn't. I have gone to some amazing places and yet been miserable. I would go on vacation and do my best to enjoy the time away, but for the most part, I failed.

My problem was that I was trying to find joy in something other than the God who made me. I sought joy in a vacation, a new electronic gadget, or an accomplishment. But none of those could

---

[55] Dennis M. Cahill, "How the Holy Spirit changed everything for me," *One Voice*, Spring 2019, 5.

[56] Charles Mathewes, "Toward a Theology of Joy," in *Joy and Human Flourishing: Essays on Theology, Culture, and the Good Life* (Minneapolis: Fortress Press, 2015), 65.

give me lasting joy, and because I didn't have joy, I couldn't *enjoy* the good things in my life.

Three months after that life-changing day in 2017, I took a Mediterranean cruise with my wife and two daughters. On that cruise, I was seeking to find my joy and satisfaction in God himself. One day, we visited the island of Capri. While my wife Patricia and oldest daughter Megan toured the island by bus, my youngest daughter Sarah and I hiked to the top of the island to see the ruins of Villa Jovis, a Roman palace built by the Roman emperor Tiberius. That day is memorable to me, not just because Sarah and I were on an island in the Mediterranean Sea but because on that day, I realized I had begun to learn how to enjoy life. Sarah and I hiked up a cobblestone path about five to six feet wide. On either side, the path was lined with Italian villas. The warm sun was shining as we walked and talked, and every once in a while, we would be startled by a break in the villas and a glorious view of the sparkling Mediterranean. On the way down, we ate lunch at a quaint Italian restaurant right on the path. It was a thoroughly enjoyable experience. If I were to choose one day in my life that I most enjoyed, it might well be that day on the Island of Capri with Sarah.

I have been to other places just as beautiful with people I love and hardly enjoyed them at all.[57] As I thought about what had made the difference, I suddenly knew: Jesus was my joy, and because he was my joy that will never pass away, I was set free to enjoy that moment on Capri. On that path, I attempted to explain to Sarah that when we find our joy in God, we are set free to enjoy the good

---

[57] My wife can attest to this sad fact.

things in life. And Sarah said, with great perception, we enjoy it "As a gift!" Exactly. Real joy is a gift from God through Jesus, and enjoyment is the gift that comes with that joy. I believe that I enjoyed that day because I had begun to find my joy and my satisfaction in God himself. Finding joy in God set me free to enjoy the gift of God—a wonder-filled day.

When we enjoy the good things God has brought into our lives, it is a kind of joy but a secondary joy. It is joy in God himself that sets us free to enjoy the good gifts he provides for us!

God made me to enjoy life. I am becoming who I was created to be.

Be joyful

How, then, do we enter into this supernatural, transcendent joy? How do we choose to be joyful people? We walk the gospel path. We live moment by moment in union with Jesus, walk by the Spirit, and submit to the will of the Father. We daily renew our hearts through the Word and prayer. We regularly build one another up in the gospel. We engage our world with the gospel in the power of the Spirit. We die to ourselves and are awakened to the resurrection life of Jesus.

God is the most joyful being in the universe. If we live in union with the joyful Jesus, by the power of the joyful Spirit, and for the glory of the Father's joy-filled agenda, we should expect to experience a transcendent joy. When joy fails us, it is like the warning light on my car dashboard: it tells me something is broken. It could be something in the world around me, but more often, it is me that is the problem. I need to realign my heart with the God of joy.

The book of Philippians is, perhaps, the book that most abounds in joy. But it does not describe comfortable lives. Paul was in prison and the Philippian church was facing persecution. And yet joy abounds, culminating in Paul's command to "rejoice in the Lord always" (Philippians 4:4). N.T. Wright tells us that Philippians is "an expression of joy and an invitation to joy."[58] If we are to experience ongoing joy, we must accept the gospel invitation to joy by living in Christ, by the Spirit, and for the glory of the Father. In the end, we must choose joy.

Our denomination's annual conference was always a challenge for me. The personal interactions were stressful, and I would be relieved when it was over. Several years ago, at one of our conferences, one pastor stopped me and said, "You look like something is wrong." I don't know what I said to him in response— maybe something like, "No, everything is fine." But the truth was that he was right. He had seen in my face the distress within. I was joyless, anxious, depressed. I was playing a role, struggling to get through.

Fast forward to another Bible Fellowship Church Conference— probably in 2019. I sat down to lunch with other church leaders, and one of the pastors, who I didn't know well, said to me, "You seem like a joyful person!" He had seen, I think, in my face the joy within. What made the difference? It wasn't anything I did; it was the fruit of God's Spirit at work in me. It was the fruit of seeking to live in union with Jesus. He observed the fruit of submitting to the will of the Father. That's the fruit of seeking to live the *gospel way*.

---

[58] N.T. Wright, "Joy: Some New Testament Perspectives and Questions," in *Joy and Human Flourishing: Essays on Theology, Culture, and the Good Life* (Minneapolis: Fortress Press, 2015), 50.

It seems to us that joy or lack of joy is thrust upon us—it happens to us. But the biblical perspective is that Christians are commanded to choose joy. But how do we do that?

- We choose joy when we think and rethink the joy-filled truths of the gospel.

- We choose joy when we intentionally live the *gospel way.*

- We choose joy when we remember our destiny—life together and forever with the God of all joy.

When the apostle Paul commands us to "Rejoice in the Lord always" (Philippians 4:4), he commands us to choose joy. So, choose to rejoice in the Lord Jesus because of who he is. Choose to rejoice in the Lord Jesus because of what he has done. Choose to rejoice in the Lord Jesus because of what he is doing. Choose to rejoice in the Lord Jesus because you will spend all eternity with him in his glorious presence. Choose joy today!

Joy is a gift that has been given in Jesus. But it is a gift we must daily seek.

The Second Fruit — A New Love

The second mark of a spiritually awakened person is a new love. This new love is first a love for Jesus that results in a life of radical obedience. Jesus says, "If you love me, you will keep my commandments."[59] The moment by moment life produces in us a new affection centered on Jesus, creating a new desire to obey.

---

[59] Cf. John 14:21, 23, 24.

But this new love is also a love for one another. Jesus said, "By this all people will know that you are my disciples, if you have love for one another" (John 13:35). The mark of the Christian is not self-righteousness or judgmentalism or keeping external rules, but a self-sacrificing love (1 Corinthians 13). In Galatians 5:22-23, when Paul recounts the fruit of the Spirit (love, joy, peace, patience, goodness, kindness, faithfulness, gentleness, and self-control), love heads the list, possibly because it embraces all the others.[60] This love is a supernatural love produced by the Spirit of God.

Harold Hoehner says love "seeks the highest good in the one loved."[61] Our problem is that since the fall of Adam and Eve, people have sought their own good above all else. But the power of the gospel is greater than our self-centeredness. As we walk *in Christ, by the Spirit, to the glory of the Father* moment by moment and as we seek daily to renew our hearts, build one another up, and engage our world with the gospel, more and more we experience the love of the Spirit poured out in us and through us (Romans 5:5).

Be second

Practically, this love is seen when Christians seek to be second as they seek to put others first. Putting others first is an act of humility. The apostle Paul says, "Do nothing from selfish ambition or conceit, but in humility count others more significant than yourselves. Let each of you look not only to his own interests, but also to the interests of others" (Philippians 2:3-4). This love is seen

---

[60] R. Alan Cole, *Galatians: An Introduction and Commentary*, vol. 9 of Tyndale New Testament Commentaries. IVP/Accordance electronic ed. (Downers Grove: InterVarsity Press, 1989), 220.

[61] Harold W. Hoehner, *Ephesians: An Exegetical Commentary* (Grand Rapids: Baker Academic, 2002), 482.

when we serve others as Jesus did.[62] To love others is to be second. To be second is to let the other have the biggest piece of cake. To be second is to watch the movie the other person wants to see rather than the one you prefer. That's the idea. I have been greatly helped by stopping and asking, "What does it mean for me to be second right now?"

When Patricia and I moved south in 2021, we bought a home with our oldest daughter, Megan. The property had a house and a separate apartment. We all shared the house, and Megan lived in the apartment. Megan is perhaps the one of our children who is most like me. Because of that, she and I have sometimes clashed, so when we bought the house together, I was concerned. I wrote up an agreement about what we would do when we might disagree. We were supposed to meet and go over our agreement at least yearly. It has been over two years and we have not needed my agreement. Why not? Because Megan and I are learning more and more to be second and to put the other first. I see this so clearly in her, and I hope she sees it in me.

The mark of the Christian is not the size of our Bibles or the beauty of our buildings. The mark of the Christian is our love. Those who are awakened to the presence, power, and purpose of the gospel are more and more living a new love. A new love is the overflow of living the *gospel way.*

The Third Fruit — A New Boldness

The last of the three marks of the spiritually awakened person is a new boldness. The apostle Paul describes the brokenness of our

---

[62] Mark 10:45 "For even the Son of Man came not to be served but to serve, and to give his life as a ransom for many."

world in Romans 8:35-36: "Who shall separate us from the love of Christ? Shall tribulation, or distress, or persecution, or famine, or nakedness, or danger, or sword? As it is written, 'For your sake we are being killed all day long; we are regarded as sheep to be slaughtered.'" The pressures and problems of life are great. There is much to fear. It is a risky world. How can we live with boldness in such a world?

In verse 37, Paul tells us, "No, in all these things we are more than conquerors through him who loved us." One commentary translates "more than conquerors" as "super-conquerors."[63] We live as "more than conquerors" through Jesus, who loved us and suffered for us. Union with the Jesus who loved us enables us to live with the boldness of conquerors.

You don't have to be a naturally bold person to experience this boldness, for this boldness is supernatural. This boldness flows from the reality of Christ in us, the Spirit at work through us, and the Father's agenda for us. In the initial days and weeks after Pentecost in Acts 2, the church, under pressure, prayed for boldness to speak the Word of God in the power of the Spirit. We read the answer to their prayer in Acts 4:31. "And when they had prayed, the place in which they were gathered together was shaken, and they were all filled with the Holy Spirit and continued to speak the word of God with boldness." The word translated "boldness" in verses 29 and 31 can mean boldness, confidence, courage, or fearlessness.[64]

---

[63] F. F. Bruce, *Romans: An Introduction and Commentary*, vol. 6 of <u>Tyndale New Testament Commentaries</u>. IVP/Accordance electronic ed. (Downers Grove: InterVarsity Press, 1985), 180.

[64] <u>*BDAG*</u>, s.v. "parrhsi÷a," 781.

How did that happen? Just a short time before, the leaders of the church, the apostles, huddled in fear. Four things happened that changed the early Christians from fearful to bold. First, they had seen Jesus. They had beheld the glory of God in the resurrected Jesus. If we are to live with a new boldness, we must intentionally seek to see the glory of God in the face of Jesus Christ (2 Corinthians 4:6). Second, they had been commissioned. The resurrected Jesus had sent them into the world with news. We will only be bold as we realize that we, too, have been commissioned to take the gospel to the people of our day. Third, the Spirit was sent. In Acts 1:8, Jesus said, "But you will receive power when the Holy Spirit has come upon you, and you will be my witnesses in Jerusalem and in all Judea and Samaria, and to the end of the earth." Only a Spirit-empowered people can live with supernatural boldness. And last, they prayed together fervently. They prayed bold prayers of risky faith — together (Acts 4:23-32).

We are not different than the people who prayed in Acts 4. We can behold Jesus moment by moment. We have been sent. The Spirit has been poured out on us. We can pray together fervently. The people of God today are called to live fearless lives in a fearful world and risky lives in a dangerous world.

Boldness does not mean being rude or uncaring. It is not arrogance or being overly self-confident. Instead, boldness is having the courage to step into the moment God gives with compassion and gentleness. We want a Spirit-given boldness!

When my daughter Megan and I traveled to Zanzibar (on a scuba diving trip), we met and befriended a wonderful family from Scotland: Tim and Sarah and their children Sophie (high school) and Adam (middle school age). During our week there, we often ate with them. We talked about scuba diving (Tim has been a diver for many years in the cold waters of Scotland, and Sophie and Adam were being certified that week), our various reading materials, and a lot about medicine (my daughter is a doctor and Sophie aspires to be a doctor), and life in general. I wanted to talk about spiritual things, but somehow, I couldn't think of a way to initiate such a conversation that didn't seem a bit awkward because I knew that parents often feel uncomfortable talking about spiritual things in the presence of their children. So, we talked about scuba diving, Scotland, work, etc. Because I couldn't think of a way to initiate a conversation, I wrongly thought Tim and Sarah weren't interested in spiritual things. On our last evening, we ate together, took pictures together, and even exchanged email addresses, but I found no opportunity to speak about the gospel. It seemed as if there would be no opportunity.

The following day, because I had to leave early, I went to breakfast early. I thought that I wouldn't even see Tim and Sarah again. But they were in the dining room (Sophie and Adam apparently slept in). I only had a little bit of time before I needed to leave. As Megan got her food, I said to Tim and Sarah, "There is a question I usually ask people... You don't have to answer if you don't want to. 'Where are you on your spiritual journey?'" They quickly responded. Tim said that since his mom's death, he had been thinking a lot about spiritual things. I listened, and Megan and I were able to share briefly what it means to be and live as a Christian. I also encouraged Tim to rekindle his faith by reading from the gospels (Tim provided the word "rekindle").

Boldness does not mean being rude or inappropriate. Sometimes, boldness means trusting God enough not to speak and then stepping into the right God-given moment.

I am not naturally bold, but the joy that I have begun to experience in Jesus and the love that flows from the Spirit and his power at work in me are producing a boldness that is not from me. It is a boldness that flows from the Spirit at work in me.

Authenticity

There is a great deal said today about being "authentic." Most of the time, when people use the word "authentic," they mean living out of their authentically broken selves. They are true to their marred character.[65] They are authentic, but it is not a godly authenticity.

The authenticity we need is being authentic to who we are in Christ. We need to live the gospel with authenticity. The great need of our day is for gospel Christians to live authentic lives of joy, love, and boldness in an often joyless, unloving, fear-filled world. The world around us needs to be amazed at Jesus in us. We are the greatest testimony to the truth of the gospel!

I watched a video called "My Adele," which is about the well-known singer by that name. In it, Adele impersonators were invited to participate in a competition in which they attempted to look like, act like, and sing like Adele. The impersonators didn't know that the real Adele was disguised as one of the competitors, identifying herself as "Jenny." Her appearance was so altered that none of the competitors recognized her as Adele. The "Adeles" began to sing

---

[65] In ourselves we are all marred by sin.

one by one, and many of them were quite good. "Jenny" was the last one scheduled to perform. While the others performed and she waited, Jenny told the others that she was very nervous. Finally, it was her turn to sing. She walked onto the stage looking very uncomfortable—so nervous that she failed to begin singing at the right time in the music. She asked for a second chance. By this point, the other competitors felt sorry for her and were hoping she didn't completely fail.

The music began to play a second time. This time, "Jenny" began to sing. She had only sung one line when one of the other competitors fell backward in her seat, flung her arms wide, and her mouth dropped open wide. She immediately knew this was the real Adele, and in short order, all of the other competitors were aware that "Jenny" was Adele. How did they know? Her voice proclaimed her authenticity. She didn't look like Adele, but only Adele could sing like that.

What was the difference between the impersonators and the real Adele? The others were playing a role. They were trying to imitate Adele, but Adele was Adele.

I have testified that for too much of my Christian life, I felt like I was playing a role: the Christian role, the pastor role. But now I seek to walk a different way: the path of Christ in me, the Spirit at work through me, and the Father's glorious purpose for me, the path of my authentic self.

The world is waiting to hear "the voice" of authentic Christians. Authentic Christians are Christians who aren't just trying to imitate Jesus, who aren't just playing a role. Christ lives in them by the power of the Spirit. They are pursuing the Father's agenda. Day by day, they renew their hearts in the gospel; day by day, they live in risky, honest community. Day by day, they engage the world with the gospel. And more and more, joy, love, and boldness are evident in their living.

The world needs to be amazed at Jesus in us. Jesus is no longer physically present, but he is present through his people, who live an authentic Christianity more and more.

A Glimpse of Glory — Jacob's Story

A testimony of God's faithfulness in my life!

My peaceful life with my wife and two children, Jerry and Joan, took an unexpected turn during our third year in church ministry. Both my wife and I were grateful to serve God. I served as an assistant pastor, and we both worked as teachers at Hope English Medium School in Shinyanga, Tanzania. In 2018, we began dreaming of planting our own church, and as we shared our vision with friends, many offered encouragement and pledged their support.

My wife had always been healthy, often teasing me about my bouts of malaria by calling me "chicken blood." I loved her lighthearted nature and the way she cared for our family. One Friday evening, when we went to the church prayer time, we discovered that the building was empty; no one had shown up. I carried our two children while she walked behind as we returned home. My wife jokingly said, "Even if I am not around, you can still care for the children."

The following day, she prepared and served breakfast and put little Joan down for a nap. But just 30 minutes later, she cried out loudly for help. Sadly, she couldn't say anything else. We rushed her to the hospital, but the doctors could only confirm that she had suffered a fatal brain stroke. Her sudden passing left me devastated and alone to care for our children. I felt abandoned, without friends or support, and I cried out to God, questioning why this had happened to me. It was a tough time.

But then, months later, in one of my darkest moments, God appeared to me in a dream, comforting me and reminding me of his greater purpose for my life. He called me to have a strong heart and assured me of His presence. I recall him saying, "Fear not! I am with you. I want to show you the purpose I have called you for." I had gone to sleep that night feeling abandoned. I awoke happy and laughing and smiling. I felt as if a heavy weight had been removed.

With God's guidance, I eventually remarried. My new wife's name is Happy. The beginning of my new marriage was difficult, but despite those difficulties, God gradually transformed our situation. We pressed on and started a new church amidst the COVID-19 pandemic, witnessing God's healing power as we ministered to broken people.

Again, tragedy happened! The new baby Happy and I were expecting died after only four days. This was a difficult time for us both. But amid my sorrow, I remembered what God had said in my dream, that he was with me and for me.

As we continued in this work of planting a church, the Lord brought supportive friends alongside us, who embraced our family and became a source of joy and companionship. Through God's grace, the sorrow that once consumed me has been replaced by joy. And Happy and I now have a new daughter, Jianna! I am humbled and grateful for God's goodness, and I am committed to serving him for the rest of my days.

Jacob Ngoko, Church Planter, Shinyanga, Tanzania

PART THREE

Ongoing Spiritual Awakening in a Broken World

≈

The gospel came into a broken world, a world of sin, pain, and suffering. The Bible tells us that the gospel of Jesus is more powerful than our world's brokenness. This part of the book explains how we live in ongoing spiritual awakening in a world gone wrong.

CHAPTER EIGHT

Life as It Ought to Be in a World That Is Not as It Ought to Be

≈

…as sorrowful, yet always rejoicing… 2 Corinthians 6:10

An obvious objection to what I have described in the previous chapters is, "What about when we experience the various afflictions, problems, distresses, and sufferings of our world?" What I have described might work well for people who are healthy and wealthy, but what about when we are neither healthy nor wealthy? How does this *gospel way* make sense of our suffering and affliction?

This world, which was created good (see Genesis 1-2), is not as it ought to be.[66] Every worldview must somehow account for the brokenness of our world. So, does this *gospel way* make sense of a world that is not as it ought to be?

In recent years, God has allowed me to walk alongside my niece Christa, my sister Cathy, and my brother-in-law Kent. In 2021, at the age of 30, Christa experienced a devastating stroke (most likely a result of the treatment she had received for a brain tumor when she was 8), which left her as a person with quadriplegia. This tragedy has been devastating for Christa and her family.

---

[66] See Cornelius Plantinga, Jr., *Not the Way It's Supposed To Be: A Breviary of Sin* (Leicester, England: William B. Eerdmans Publishing Company, 1995).

In 2022, my wife and I drove to Fort Lauderdale to be with Christa, Cathy, and Kent shortly after they learned that it had been a stroke that had disabled her (doctors originally thought that her disability had a different cause). I did not know why we were going there; I just knew we needed to go. We rented a small place at the Fort Lauderdale beach near their home. The first night we were there, Cathy, Kent, and Christa came down to where we were staying, and we ate dinner sitting at one of the outside tables overlooking the ocean. After dinner, I said we should pray. Although I wasn't sure exactly why we had come, I assumed that one purpose was to pray for Christa, so we held an impromptu prayer time. At the end, with all the faith that I had, I prayed for Christa: that God would miraculously heal her.

I finished my prayer. But Christa wasn't healed. Through tears, she said, "God is never going to heal me!" I didn't know what to say. But what I thought was, "Lord, I am done with that. You called me to pray for her, and I did. I will serve Christa and her family this week in any way I can, but I am done praying aloud for her. I did not come here to make her cry." And that is what I did throughout the week. Every day, I went to their home. I brought coffee and donut holes. I helped the therapist with the therapy.

My 50th high school class reunion coincided with the end of our week in Fort Lauderdale. I had never been to a reunion before, and Patricia and I had decided that we would attend this one since we would be in Fort Lauderdale anyway. At the reunion, I was reacquainted with Bob, a former classmate, and as we enjoyed the reunion dinner, I overheard Bob tell someone at our table the story of his daughter Kylie. Kylie had been growing progressively blind but was miraculously healed (see Kylie's story at the end of this chapter). As Bob told Kylie's story, I was filled with emotion. "Lord, what does this mean for me and praying for Christa?" The following day was Sunday, and Patricia and I planned to worship online with Kent, Cathy, and Christa at their home, along with Christa's sister, Kaitlyn, and her husband, Ben. Surely, it was not a coincidence that I had heard Kylie's story at the reunion. But what did it mean? What was I to do?

We gathered in Kent and Cathy's home the following day to participate in the Sunday morning online service. I was still filled with emotion, along with a sense that God wanted me to say and do something. But what? After the online service, I asked if I could say a few words (the downside of having a brother who is a pastor!), and I shared a few thoughts from Romans 8. We live in a groaning world, I said (Romans 8:22-23). They could all identify with that. But there is hope (Romans 8:24-25), and there is help (the Spirit prays for us, Romans 8:26-27). All things ultimately work together for our good (Romans 8:28), I said—even quadriplegia. And then I said I would like to pray for Christa again. So, I placed my hands on her shoulders and prayed. I sought to pray "by the Spirit" (Ephesians 6:18; Jude 20) and to pray with faith and zeal. I prayed that God would heal Christa. I prayed that God would do a miracle. But when I ended my prayer, again, Christa wasn't healed.

Why did God choose to heal Kylie and not Christa? Did I need to pray louder or with more faith? Did I need to express more emotion? Did I say the right words? Was it that I do not have the gift of healing? I do not have all the answers. But here is what I do know: God loves both Kylie and Christa with a love that is beyond our understanding (Ephesians 3:19). God is able to heal. It is right to seek healing. God always does what is right. But he does not always heal. For reasons we cannot understand on this side of eternity, he heals some for his glory, and he allows others not to be healed—also for his glory.

Kylie's healing is a great story of the power of God. The miracle of her healing reminds us that God is amazing. But I believe learning to live with the challenges of quadriplegia with contentment and even, at times, with joy, is a greater miracle. It, too, reminds us that God is amazing.

The Path of Affliction

We live in a broken world. Theologians often discuss the "already" and the "not yet" of the gospel. This age is "already" the time of fulfillment. The Messiah has come, and the Spirit has been given (Acts 2). Jesus came so that we might live life to the fullest (John 10:10). The Kingdom of God is here.

But all of God's promises have "not yet" been fully fulfilled. People still get cancer; and relationships are broken. A husband loses his job. Jesus said, "In the world you will have tribulation" (John 16:33). Our joy is often mixed with sorrow. In Acts 14:22, Paul and Barnabas told the church that "through many tribulations we must enter the kingdom of God." The Christian experience is lived out in the midst of great suffering, persecution, and difficulty. The Kingdom of God has "not yet" come in its fullness.

To walk the *gospel way,* we must embrace both the "already" *and* the "not yet" of the gospel. We do not deny the brokenness of our world. And yet we are to live by faith as "more than conquerors" (Romans 8:37) amid a broken world. The Kingdom has come, and yet the Kingdom has not yet come fully. The gospel is good news in a bad-news world.

The brokenness of our world is the context in which we must live the wonder-filled promises of the gospel. We are to live the "supernaturalness" of the gospel in a world gone wrong. The apostle Peter describes the normal Christian experience in chapter 1 of his first epistle (emphasis added in bold):

³Blessed be the God and Father of our Lord Jesus Christ! According to his great mercy, he has caused us to be born again to a living hope through the resurrection of Jesus Christ from the dead, ⁴to an inheritance that is imperishable, undefiled, and unfading, kept in heaven for you, ⁵who by God's power are being guarded through faith for a salvation ready to be revealed in the last time. ⁶In this you rejoice, though now for a little while, if necessary, **you have been grieved by various trials**, ⁷so that the tested genuineness of your faith—more precious than gold that perishes though it is tested by fire—may be found to result in praise and glory and honor at the revelation of Jesus Christ. ⁸Though you have not seen him, you love him. Though you do not now see him, **you believe in him and rejoice with joy that is inexpressible and filled with glory,** ⁹obtaining the outcome of your faith, the salvation of your souls. (1 Peter 1:3-9).

Notice the words I have highlighted in bold. We are "grieved by various trials." This is characteristic of the broken world in which we live. The kingdom is "not yet." Yet, because we believe in him, we "rejoice with joy that is inexpressible and filled with glory." That refers to the "already-ness" of our day. The Kingdom has come in Jesus. There is joy even in our sorrow.

To live life as God intends, we must focus on the "already-ness" of this age of fulfillment. We must look past the anguish of our day to the powerful presence of Christ in us by the Spirit. I am beginning to understand that in this broken world, affliction is not a hindrance to *life as it ought to be*; it is the path of *life as it ought to be!* Life's difficulties are not a roadblock to the abundant life but rather the road on which we walk the abundant life. Jesus walked the path of suffering, and we follow in his footsteps. *Life as it ought to be*, then, is the life of faith lived out in a world of brokenness.

Living the *Gospel Way* in a Broken World

But how do we do that? How do we live with joy, particularly when some suffering is so overwhelming?

Here is what I have come to believe: if living the *gospel way* only works for people who are healthy, then it doesn't work. But it does work. The apostle Paul put it this way: "...sorrowful yet always rejoicing" (2 Corinthians 6:10). James 1:2 makes the stunning statement: "Count it all joy, my brothers, when you meet trials of various kinds..." I believe that those facing overwhelming suffering can experience *life as it ought to be*. *Life as it ought to be* is not an easy life; it is just a better life.

How does walking the *gospel way* transform our sufferings? Walking the *gospel way* transforms our sufferings by changing our perspective. As we walk the *gospel way*, we begin to understand three things.

1. It is in our suffering that we most experience the presence of Jesus.

Why? Because Jesus was a man of sorrows (Isaiah 53:3). Jesus understands suffering, and we understand Jesus better as we walk the path of sorrow. Paul said his greatest desire was "that I may know him and the power of his resurrection, and may share his sufferings, becoming like him in his death" (Philippians 3:10). We draw near to Jesus in our affliction. We need to understand our suffering as sharing in his suffering.

My friend Phil Morrison was a pastor and then a missionary in Kenya, Africa.[67] Phil says that in his years as a pastor and missionary, it always felt like Jesus was there but in the next room. His relationship had always been a cerebral and intellectual one. He wanted an emotional connection and a "relational relationship" with Jesus but could not connect emotionally with the Lord. Then, he wrote his doctoral dissertation on child abuse in Africa, and it brought him into contact with some of the darkest aspects of humanity. He couldn't simply deal with abuse on an academic level. He didn't know what to do with the emotions this darkness created in his soul. When Morrison told another missionary of his distress, the missionary asked, "Have you tried the practice of lament?" So, Phil began to express his deep sorrow over the loss of innocence that so many children had experienced. God used this experience to help Phil begin to connect with him emotionally. As Phil did that—as he poured out his heart to God in sorrow—the door opened for him to enter the same room as Jesus and experience his presence and comfort on a real and personal level.

Jesus is there to meet our needs when we draw near to him in our suffering. And when we draw near to him, he draws near to us.

---

[67] Dr. Philip E. Morrison is the author of several books, *including Conflict Resolution in the Church; Mastering Ministry: Key Principles for Every Pastor;* and *Falling Asleep in the Lap of Delilah: Lessons on Finishing Well from the Life of Samson.* Phil tells this story in his most recent book *In The Same Room As Jesus: Entering a Deeper Friendship with Christ* (India: Oasis International Publishing, 2023).

2. It is in our suffering that we most experience the power of Jesus.

In 2 Corinthians 12, the apostle cried out to God three times, asking him to remove the "thorn" in his flesh. Many believe this "thorn" was probably some physical ailment, though there is no universally accepted consensus. I think that Paul left his ailment vague so we can apply it to our many ailments and life challenges. Listen to Paul's conclusion in verses 8-10:

[8]Three times I pleaded with the Lord about this, that it should leave me. [9]But he said to me, "My grace is sufficient for you, for my power is made perfect in weakness." Therefore, I will boast all the more gladly of my weaknesses, so that the power of Christ may rest upon me. [10]For the sake of Christ, then, I am content with weaknesses, insults, hardships, persecutions, and calamities. For when I am weak, then I am strong.

Paul was content in his affliction because it was in that affliction that he more fully experienced Jesus' power and presence.

3. It is in our suffering that we most experience the Father's good purpose for us.

The path of the gospel is the path of affliction. Our afflictions are not a hindrance to God's purpose for us; they are the means by which God's purpose is fulfilled in us. Christ went to the cross, and God's purposes were fulfilled in his suffering. It is so for us. Romans 8:28 is crucial to our understanding: "And we know that for those who love God all things work together for good, for those who are called according to his purpose."

The gospel is always good news for the people of God. As I have already said, the gospel is good news in a bad-news world.

I recall visiting someone from our church who was dying of cancer. The doctors had nothing more they could do for her; all they had was bad news. But whenever I visited her, I would say, "I have good news for you!" and read to her one of the joyful promises of the gospel. One time, shortly before she died, she asked me, as I walked into her room, and before I could say anything to her, "What's the good news?" And I had good and joy-filled news for her! I spoke of the life to come, which the apostle Paul tells us in Philippians 1:23 is "far better."

Because the gospel is good news, those who walk the gospel path can boast in their sufferings, as Paul declares in Romans 5:

³Not only that, but we rejoice in our sufferings, knowing that suffering produces endurance, ⁴and endurance produces character, and character produces hope, ⁵and hope does not put us to shame, because God's love has been poured into our hearts through the Holy Spirit who has been given to us. (Romans 5:3-5)

The word translated "rejoice" in verse 3 is often translated as "boast." We can boast in our sufferings as we walk the path of the gospel. We don't boast about the sufferings themselves, but we boast in our God, who is able to bring good out of our suffering. And as we boast in our sufferings, our sufferings begin to lose their power over us.

I visited with my good friends Frank and Veronika Sarcone a few years ago. Frank was a retired fireman, pastor, and counselor, and in their retirement years, Frank and Veronika became part of Christ Community Church. Frank's health was fragile and had been so for some time. There had been multiple hospital stays. Just before my visit, Frank had broken his femur due to his treatments, which was very painful for him. But Frank and Veronika were such a joy to visit. During my visit, I asked Frank, "Tell me how you have joy in such affliction?"

Frank started talking about his sufferings, and there was a lot to tell. But then he abruptly stopped and said, "There is a God. I am a child of the king," lifting his fist in victory as he spoke. What was he doing? He was boasting in the Lord in his affliction.

Suffering is the context in which God's presence, power, and purpose is most fully experienced. The path of those who live the *gospel way* is a path that includes suffering. The light of the gospel shines most brightly in the darkness of our affliction. We are called to live *in Christ, by the Spirit,* and *to the glory of the Father* in a broken world.

Over the years, God has allowed me to experience some affliction, though I have to add that many have experienced affliction much greater than mine. In the 1990s, I walked with my wife Patricia through the uncertainty of a serious breast cancer diagnosis. It hit me "like a ton of bricks." I was overwhelmed by the thought of losing her. I have walked the path of anxiety and depression (see Chapter 1). My emotions, at times, have been broken. I have (and sometimes still do) experienced what has been called "the dark night of the soul."[68] As my wife and I have aged, we have begun to face the various weaknesses and afflictions of aging.

---

[68] The phrase "the dark night of the soul" comes from a poem by St. John of the Cross.

In writing this chapter, I have tried to live the *gospel way* by remembering that my afflictions are the path I must walk if I want to follow in Jesus' footsteps. They are the way I most experience the presence, power, and purpose of the gospel. They are not a hindrance to what God wants to do in me and through me. Rather, they are the path I must walk if God's purposes are to be fulfilled in me.

We aren't to seek affliction. We try to alleviate suffering in ourselves and others as much as possible. We thank God for doctors, hospitals, and all who care for the suffering. We cry out to a compassionate God for relief. We genuinely lament the real losses that we experience. But when God allows affliction into our lives, we seek to endure it and embrace it in the power of the Spirit. And then, by the power of the Spirit in us, it is possible to even boast in our sufferings! And, yes, it is possible to "rejoice with joy that is inexpressible and filled with glory" (1 Peter 1:8) in the various trials that God allows.

None of us likes adversity. But adversity keeps us from superficiality. It keeps us from a life of insignificance. It is in adversity that the story of the gospel is played out in our lives. All the great stories contain adversity. Without great adversity, there are no great stories. Your story is a great story for your story is a story of gospel adversity. In the adversities of your life, the presence of Christ is experienced, the power of the Spirit is demonstrated, and the purpose of the Father is fulfilled.

I have discovered that when I find my joy in God himself, I am able to enjoy the good things in life that God brings and am better able to endure the difficult things that he allows. I have discovered that when I find my joy in God himself, I am even able to embrace my suffering.

Embrace Your Suffering

None of us likes adversity, and we aren't to seek adversity. But when God allows adversity into our lives, we are to embrace it. But what does it mean to embrace suffering?

- **We embrace our suffering theologically** — (1) We understand that God has a good purpose in whatever affliction he allows into our lives (Romans 8:28). Our suffering is a consequence of what theologians call "the fall," the moment when sin entered our world (Genesis 3). But God is able to use our suffering for his good (Romans 8:28). And (2) we look forward to the last day when there will be no more tears or death, no more mourning, crying or pain for the former things will have passed away. (Revelation 21:4)

- **We embrace our suffering emotionally** — In our suffering, we draw near to Jesus, the man of sorrows. With the apostle Paul, we yearn to know him and his resurrection power and begin to see our sufferings as sharing in the sufferings of Jesus (Philippians 3:10). In our suffering, we "step into the same room as Jesus."

- **We embrace our suffering verbally** — We boast in our afflictions (Romans 5:5). We declare that we are more than conquerors in a broken world (Romans 8:37). We speak God's truth about our sufferings. We preach the gospel to ourselves.

Embracing our sufferings is not easy or immediate. It is most often a process that may take months or years. As we walk the hard path of embracing our suffering, we discover that our suffering begins to lose its power over us little by little.

Conclusion

Everyone has a philosophy of life. We all seek to make sense of our world in different ways. Every philosophy of life must account for the reality of suffering and affliction. If a philosophy of life doesn't work when someone is in a hospital bed dying of cancer…it just doesn't work.

But the *gospel way*, a life lived *in Christ, by the Spirit, to the glory of the Father*, does work. It works in every situation if we will embrace it. The *gospel way* is not an easy path, but it is the path that gives hope and even joy in the face of suffering, affliction, persecution, and death.

And that is *life as it ought to be.*

A Glimpse of Glory — Kylie's Story

Kylie was diagnosed in 2019 with an eye disease called Retinitis Pigmentosa (RP), a rare genetic eye disease that causes most who have it to go completely blind. She was told that there is no cure for RP. At her diagnosis, Kylie had lost 58% of her vision in one eye and 42% in the other. After her devastating diagnosis, Kylie's vision steadily worsened. She lost her night vision and increasingly lost her peripheral vision. She was preparing to live for Jesus as a blind person.

In 2020, a counselor challenged Kylie to seek healing from God. She was told to read the Gospels and Acts and note each story of healing. Up until that point, she had not asked God to heal her vision. This is Kylie's story—in her own words.

In 2021, I went to North Carolina for an eye appointment. My Uber driver picked me up, his accent thick from the heart of Africa. I asked him which country he was from. "Nigeria," he responded. We chatted about Africa for a moment before he asked me if North Carolina was my home or if I was visiting. "Both, actually," I said. I told him that I had lived in North Carolina but now lived in Atlanta and was back in North Carolina for an eye appointment. He asked me to explain. I told him my diagnosis and prognosis. He waited momentarily and responded, "You will not go blind; you will ask, and your sight will be restored. You will eat from a garden, and you will see." In that moment, I was both shaken and confused. Did he not understand the science of it all? Or did he just have a faith that was bigger than mine? I texted my group of girlfriends about it and then somehow promptly forgot the interchange.

My eye appointment brought more news. At each appointment since my diagnosis, my eye pressures had crept higher and higher and were headed toward a dangerous range of pressures. My doctor explained that RP caused the pressure to increase at each appointment. My pressure had risen from 14 at diagnosis to 21-22 at that appointment.

Back home in Atlanta, the pandemic dragged on. I was longing to find new community and was desperate to be "in person" with other believers talking about Jesus. I greatly desired to find other believers to join me in the wrestling place where I found myself. I heard of an in-person Bible study that was starting in February. Though it was over an hour's drive from my house, I didn't care. I began to attend the study, and God used it to open the eyes of my heart, enabling me to see a "bigness" of him that I had not previously experienced.

Week after week, I found myself blowing up the walls of the box I had unknowingly placed God in. I was digging into the Bible and prayer like never before. I was still wrestling with the question of whether to seek healing even as I was seeing Scripture in a new way. Meanwhile, I was still working my way from Matthew to Acts, and the Holy Spirit was coming to life for me in fresh, new ways.

For the final week of the Bible study, the leaders (whom we had been watching on video) would be present in person. As I made my hour-long drive, I figured they might ask if we had any questions or areas of the study we wanted to talk about, and as I drove, I prepared my litany of questions. "What about the people who don't get healed? Why do people seemingly have to ask for healing? Why wouldn't God just zap down healing without us needing to participate in some way? And if I have to participate, that feels like it's my responsibility… shouldn't I be trying to get away from a faith based on performance?"

Questions swirled as I tried to remember all I had struggled with as I made my way through the miracles of Jesus and the disciples. As I listed them in my mind while driving on I-85, God clearly said, "Let it go. You can stop wrestling. Open your hands and ask me." It immediately felt like a new revelation. My thoughts immediately changed—a complete 180-degree turn. Why in the world was I wrestling this to the ground? I didn't want my cynicism, skepticism, or lack of full understanding about healing to be the block to just saying "yes" to God's invitation. Each time I read another miracle of Jesus and another healing story, it was as if I heard God say, "Just ask me; you are my beloved daughter, so you can ask." But each time, I came up with three reasons why I couldn't ask God; fears and misunderstandings would keep me from truly asking for healing. But then, right there on the Interstate, I told God I was finished wrestling; I was ready to receive. I was ready to ask—not because I was somehow deserving but because of my position as his daughter.

So I asked, as plainly and confidently as I could, "God heal me. I believe you can, and I am your daughter asking her Father for something you've told me to ask you. I don't understand it, and I don't have to, but I trust you and know you're able. Jesus, heal my eyes."

Honestly, it was an easy prayer to ask after I finally got to the place of release and receiving, and it was far less lofty or weighty than I imagined it would be. It came and went far more quickly than all the wrestling, and I went on to sing and pray my way up the Interstate until I arrived at the final gathering of our Bible study.

I had never met Rachel or Karen (the study's authors) before, but I immediately sensed the Spirit in their presence. They taught the last lesson, which was all about the explosive, transformative power of the Spirit and how often we miss out because we don't know to ask for more. They mentioned the previous week's homework, part of which was a fill-in-the-blank prayer we were supposed to ask of God. No one volunteered to share their prayer, but I was immediately prompted to share mine. Here's what I read:

"Dear Beloved Daughter, I am so pleased that you are leaning into all that I am. I have been waiting for you to see me in a new light—to come with me to a deeper place. You have been mistaken when you thought that I was a punishing, displeased, or unwilling Father. I can't wait for you to soak in all that I am and see the invitations I have set before you."

As I read it aloud, while I didn't remember a single word that I had written down, my heart rang true with each word. I had heard so clearly from the Lord that this diagnosis was never about the outcome. Instead, he took what the enemy meant for evil and used it for my good—as a way to take me to a deeper place with him, a place I couldn't get to without his aid. He had put invitation after invitation before me along this journey of losing my vision, and as I—sometimes boldly and sometimes reluctantly—said "yes" to each one, it made way for another invitation. My spiritual eyes were opening with each passing week, and I was seeing him in a new light. I was seeing his Word in a way that was alive and inviting and so very intimate. I was not reading words on a page or eyewitness accounts of miracles; I was hearing the words of a Father who wanted to reach his daughter's heart.

Karen looked at me and said, "Can we pray for you?" I welcomed it. Karen, Rachel, and the four facilitators of our study gathered around me and began to pray. Rachel mentioned first healing for my eyes: for them to be opened in radical fullness and for the healing Christ died for to come forth into that moment. Karen paused and asked if I had a diagnosis. As I explained what it was, she came, put her hand on my eyes, and began to pray that my diagnosis of blindness would come under the power of Jesus. She asked that by faith, I would receive my sight, and she commanded that my vision be expanded.

She asked if I could see, but as I opened my eyes, my vision was unchanged. I saw what I usually did. I told her that I could see perfectly when I looked straight ahead and that, thus far, I had only lost my peripheral vision. Putting my hands up near my cheeks, I told her I could see to a certain point but no further. "Then we are not done praying," she replied, and she put her hand on each of my hands and continued to pray as she pushed my hands back toward the spot near my shoulders, where my peripheral vision ended. Immediately as she pushed my hands, color, light, and clarity rushed into my peripheral vision as each person in the room came into striking clarity beside me. As I looked into Karen's eyes, I felt a sense of disorientation as my sight was suddenly expanding. First, I saw one lady on the couch…then another…then another…then the table and lamp…then my friend directly to my right. I could see her ponytail, jacket, and glasses with sharp clarity.

It was shocking, overwhelming, amazing, surprising, and awe-invoking. I had not realized how small my vision had become until that moment when it became expansive in an instant. I had gone from looking through what felt like a toilet paper tube to being in an IMAX theater. Everything felt completely huge and overwhelming. For the last two years, I would "test myself" all the time to see how much vision I had. I would put my hands up in my periphery and see when they came into view. I knew exactly how close my hand needed to reach my cheek before seeing it. There I sat, hands out above my shoulders, and I could see both hands completely. It was unavoidably, unexplainably, and inextricably miraculous.

I got in the car to drive home after the miracle and sat in the driver's seat. I stared at the car in front of me and was floored at all I could see: my cup in the cup holder, my gear shifter, my jeans, my door handles, and locks—it was almost distracting how much I could see! I moved my hands around like a crazy person, and not once did they go out of my view. I drove home weeping. I called my husband John, my parents, and my sister and told them. I was in complete amazement at all God had done—at the Spirit's healing work.

The next day, I made an appointment with a local eye doctor's office to ask if they would do a retinal scan. I drove to the doctor's office, wondering what they would say. I thought that somehow, my experience of sight had changed, but perhaps not the physical scans. The nurse tested the pressure in my eyes at the doctor's office. Before, my pressures had gone from 14 (normal) at the time of diagnosis to 21-22 at my last appointment. The nurse said, "Your pressures are 14, in the normal range." What? My pressure went down seven points! The nurse then took me to retinal imaging, where they conducted various scans of my eyes. When the doctor came in, he looked at the scans and explained that RP is a disease that causes retinal cells, rods, and cones to die, and it shows up on a retinal cell as black speckling on the retina. Then he pulled up my images and said, "These scans are not congruent with someone with RP; there is no evident retinal cell death on these scans."

A month later, I went back to Duke Eye Center, where they had first done the litany of tests, and they tested my eyes. My doctor stumbled through six scans that were different than January, last July, and all of 2019. The five edemas [swellings]—absent from the scans. He sat there stuttering, explaining that RP degrades or thins the retinal cell wall but mine had *thickened* since January. Large portions of the retinal cell wall were healed—back to a more normal thickness. I explained to him that this was due to the power of prayer and only by Jesus. He responded, "Well, that is an intangible I can't measure."

Isn't this our God? Isn't he bigger than we think? More powerful than we know? He is still the God who heals.

CHAPTER NINE

Crying Out in a Broken World

〜

And this is the confidence that we have toward him, that if we ask anything according to his will he hears us. And if we know that he hears us in whatever we ask, we know that we have the requests that we have asked of him. 1 John 5:14-15

On that day in February 2017, I was crying out to God in prayer. I experienced spiritual renewal through the Word of God as I prayed. My awakening came through prayer! This is not surprising because when we pray, we step into the realm of the supernatural.

The writers of the psalms often "cried" to God. They didn't just pray; they cried out to God in desperation (Psalm 18:6). In their desperation, they saw God as their only hope. I call prayer "the desperate cry of desperate people." The only way to live in a broken world is to cry out to the God who hears.

Pray Without Ceasing

1 Thessalonians 5:17 tells us to "pray without ceasing." But what could that mean? I think it means…to pray without ceasing! This seems impossible to us, but consider the young man in love. He says about his beloved, "I think about her all the time." And he does. He thinks about her when he wakes and when he goes to work; he calls her on his breaks, and he ponders her beauty as he drives home from work. She is on his mind as he drifts off to sleep. He thinks about

her without ceasing. We must pray without ceasing. We must pray when we rise, when we work, when we play. We must turn our living into an ongoing conversation with the God who loves us.

Pray about everything. Pray when things are going well and pray when things are falling apart. Pray about big things and small things. In prayer, we encounter the God who is able. We live in a broken world. It is not broken once in a while; it is broken all the time. And so, we must pray without ceasing.

Pray Personally

We must pray as individuals. I pray before I arise in the morning, before my daily Bible reading, and as I read the Bible. I seek to pray throughout my day, about everything. We must have set prayer times, but we must also pray spontaneously throughout the day. We must cultivate the habit of praying all the time.

Pray Together

God's people not only cry out to him personally; we are told to pray together. In the book of Acts, we see numerous times when the people of God came together to pray (Acts 1:14; 4:24; 12:5,12). Prayer is powerful. God unleashes his power when the people of God pray together. One reason the church of Jesus Christ has often been ineffective in responding to the pressures of our age is that we have lost the art of praying together.

I once attended a church prayer meeting where only a few people gathered. I remarked, "The nice thing about a prayer meeting is that you can always get a parking place." But that is not always true. Another time, I went with some of our church leaders to the prayer meeting at the Brooklyn Tabernacle in New York City.

We had been advised to arrive early to get a good seat. It turned out to be good advice. The large audience had gathered, not for entertainment, but to pray. It is not a wonder that the Brooklyn Tabernacle experiences the power of God!

Pray Expecting the Supernatural

The prayer of faith is a prayer that expects God to answer. It is a prayer that expects God to do more than we ask or imagine (Ephesians 3:20). It is a prayer that expects the supernatural. It is a prayer that seeks God's glory above all else.

Recently, my niece Christa asked me, "If God already knows what we will pray for, why do we pray?" My best answer is that prayer is communion with God; it is a conversation with God. In prayer, we step into his supernatural presence. Prayer is about God but for us. We pray not to let God know what we need but so that we will know that God knows. In prayer, we experience intimacy with God.

The Pattern for Prayer

In Matthew 6:9-13, Jesus gives us a pattern for believing prayer.[69] I follow this pattern in my personal prayer and when I lead others in praying.

We begin with God: "Our Father in heaven, hallowed be your name."

We surrender to God: "Your kingdom come, your will be done, on earth as it is in heaven."

[69] Daniel Henderson, *Transforming Prayer: How Everything Changes When You Seek God's Face* (Minneapolis: Bethany House Publishers, 2011), 162.

We ask from God: "Give us this day our daily bread, forgive us our debts, as we also have forgiven our debtors."

We walk with God: "And lead us not into temptation but deliver us from evil."

This simple pattern allows for almost unlimited diversity. This approach to prayer is worship-based (we begin with God), Scripture-fed (we always pray out of the Bible), and Spirit-led (we seek the spontaneous direction of the Spirit: see Ephesians 6:18; Jude 20).[70]

The Mystery of Prayer

We sometimes say that prayer is a mystery. Why are some prayers answered and some are not? In 1 John 5:14-15, we discover the answer. "And this is the confidence that we have toward him, that if we ask anything according to his will, he hears us. And if we know that he hears us in whatever we ask, we know that we have the requests that we have asked of him." It is not that prayer is a mystery. Prayer is simple. God answers the fervent, believing prayers of his people that are according to his will. It is the will of God that is often a mystery! God has revealed his will to us in broad outlines: he is rescuing a people for his glory. But we most often do not know the details of God's will. If we could see things from the perspective of eternity, we would see that God always answers the cries of faith that are according to his will.

This helps explain other passages about prayer. I believe that abiding in him as we pray (John 15:7), praying in Jesus' name (John 15:16), and praying according to his will (1 John 5:14) are essentially saying the same thing. When we abide in him, and his words abide

---

[70] Henderson, *Old Paths,* 125.

in us, we are seeking his will to be done. When we pray "in his name," we are praying as representatives of Jesus who seek his will, not our own. Why doesn't God always give us what we ask? God knows better.

My wife and I once watched a movie about someone who always had every prayer answered just as he asked. Let's just say that it didn't go well for him. Since then, Patricia and I have often remarked to one another that we are thankful that God doesn't always answer our prayers (at least not as we ask)!

Thus, it is always right to pray, "Not my will be done, but your will be done," as Jesus did. Often, we don't know God's will for a particular moment, but sometimes God gives us faith that says to the mountain (a metaphor for things that seem impossible), "Move from here to there" (Matthew 17:20), and we can pray with great freedom and confidence.

As I have said, my daughter Megan and I have taken up scuba diving. We were diving in Islamorada in the Florida Keys a few years ago. One night, we went for a night dive, but Megan had a problem with seasickness. It was not pleasant for her. The following day, before our next dive, I arose early, as usual, and went to the beach to read the Bible and pray.

It was windy that day; a breeze almost always comes off the Atlantic Ocean. But as I sat on my lounge chair to read, it was not just a breeze but a strong wind: so windy that I tried to think of somewhere else on the property to go for my reading—somewhere not so windy. And then I thought, "If Megan had a problem with seasickness last night and today it is this windy, she will get seasick again. Then she won't want to dive anymore, and I will lose my dive partner."

And then, as best I can remember, I prayed. It wasn't a great, power-filled, faith-filled, passionate prayer. It was just a pray-without-ceasing, pray-about-everything, small-faith prayer for Megan and her seasickness. And then...the wind died down. It didn't just die down; it became completely still. There was not a hint of wind. I thought to myself, "That's interesting." I went back to the room, told my wife and Megan what had happened, and we prepared for a day of scuba diving.

When we got to the small harbor where the boat was moored, I noticed how still the water was. Instead of the usual light chop, it was like a lake—not a ripple. We went diving and had a wonderful day.

The following day, we went diving again. Before we embarked, I was talking with someone and mentioned how good the weather had been the previous day. He said, "Yes, but the weather was only good right here."

What do I make of all that? Could it all be coincidence? I suppose. But I don't believe it. I think that God answered my small-faith prayer. But why? Why would God answer something as insignificant as a scuba diving prayer but seemingly not answer so many much more important prayers? My best answer is that God was saying, "See my power? See the power of prayer?" God was teaching me that even a prayer of small faith could unleash the power of the creator of the universe. God was teaching me that I must daily align my heart with his will, abide in him, and pray in his name. I must learn to pray without ceasing. And he will accomplish his will in me and through me in accordance with his will and in his time.

Conclusion

If we are to live the *gospel way* in a world of brokenness, we must learn to pray without ceasing, to pray personally, and to pray together. We must learn to pray expecting the supernatural.

I have often prayed, "I don't know how to pray. Lord, teach me to pray." But I may need to stop asking that, for God has taught me how to pray. He has given me a pattern, shown me his power, given me the Spirit, and told me to pray with my brothers and sisters. Praying without ceasing, seeking his will, and crying out in our need is how we live in a broken world. It is how we step into *life as it ought to be.*

CHAPTER TEN

Living This Day for That Day

～

> *The Christian is a man who can be certain about the ultimate*
> *even when he is most uncertain about the immediate.* [71] *Dr.*
> *Martyn Lloyd Jones*

I said in Chapter 5 that we can only live in this one moment. That is true. But we are always to live this one moment in light of the future. Too often, we focus almost exclusively on the future of this present age. We think of the meeting after lunch, our hope for marriage or promotion, our fear of sickness and death, or our upcoming retirement. However, Christians must learn to focus more and more on the eternal future. We always live on the edge of eternity. Therefore, we must live *this day for that day*. We must live this one day in light of that day when we will stand before Jesus.

There are two aspects to *living this day for that day:*

We Seek to Please Him on That Day

"So, whether we are at home or away, we make it our aim to please him. For we must all appear before the judgment seat of Christ, so that each one may receive what is due for what he has done in the body, whether good or evil" (2 Corinthians 5:9,10).

---

[71] Martin Lloyd-Jones, "God in Control: a Sermon on Romans 8:28-30," mljtrust.org, https://www.mljtrust.org/sermons/book-of-romans/god-in-control-2/.

There is a judgment of works even for the Christian. This does not contradict the Bible idea of justification (being made right with God) by grace alone. "There is therefore now no condemnation for those who are in Christ Jesus" (Romans 8:1). The judgment of works on the last day will be the evidence that we have experienced the grace of God. Our salvation is always based only on the grace of God.

For the Christian, the desire to please God because we will give account is a product of and evidence for the grace of God at work in us. We seek to please our loving heavenly Father the way a child seeks to please her loving father by cleaning her room, knowing that Dad will be home soon. We are to seek to live now in a way that will please him on that day. He will not condemn us should we fail, yet to please him is our greatest desire.

The first part of this book told the story of how I automatically and most often unconsciously sought to please other people, to earn their approval. This was disastrous for me spiritually, morally, and emotionally. The gospel set me free and has begun to create a desire to please him above everyone and everything. This is true freedom.

To please him should be the greatest yearning of our hearts, not just in theory but in reality. We live this day for that day because we yearn to hear him say on the last day, "Well done, good and faithful servant" (Matthew 25:21).

I have found it very helpful to reframe my thinking or potential words or actions from the perspective of the last day when I will give account. I imagine myself standing before Jesus, explaining a certain decision or action. This way of thinking creates within me a desire to please him on that day rather than to please people in this day. I ask, "Will what I am about to do or say please Jesus on the last day?"

A while ago, I was writing an email to someone I care about. I wanted to admit that I hadn't handled a situation quite right. I found myself trying to write the email in a way that would please my friend, and that would present me in a good light. The right words didn't seem to come. Then I thought about it like this: One day, I will stand before Jesus and give an account for the words of that email. Will what I write please Jesus? And as I thought about that, I knew just what I needed to say. Instead of seeking to please my friend (not unimportant), my greatest desire became to please Jesus on that last day when I share in his glory and beauty. I saw the email from the perspective of eternity rather than the perspective of this passing away moment.

We Live in Anticipation of That Day

The glory we will share is far greater than we can imagine. Two verses specially make that point:

- "For I consider that the sufferings of this present time are not worth comparing with the glory that is to be revealed to us" (Romans 8:18).

- "For this light momentary affliction is preparing for us an eternal weight of glory beyond all comparison..." (2 Corinthians 4:17).

We live in anticipation of *that day*, which is far better. This "living hope" (1 Peter 1:3) enables us to endure difficult things and enjoy life's good things. The more we experience the brokenness of *this day*, the more we yearn for the glory of *that day*.

"No eye has seen, no ear has heard, and no mind has imagined what God has prepared for those who love him." 1 Corinthians: 2:9

We can only live this one moment. We are to live this one moment in the present, but always in anticipation of that day when we will step into Jesus' glory and with the awareness that we will give account to him. We begin to experience *life as it ought to be* when we anticipate *life as it will be.*

How Do We Live This Day for That Day?

We reframe our thinking. We ask ourselves, "What will I say to Jesus on the last day about the actions, words, and decisions I am about to make today?" This reframing enables us to see life from an eternal perspective and to seek to please him more than people.

We live in anticipation of that day. One day soon (and the life to come is always "soon"), we will be with him for all eternity. Becoming more aware of the wonder of that day means I can better deal with today's brokenness.

I am now 70 years of age. Patricia and I are beginning to experience some of the decline accompanying older age. I often feel the weight of that. Yet, we are on the edge of venturing into a new ministry.[72] As I write these words, I am preparing to travel to Tanzania to present the information in this book to a group of Tanzanian pastors. It will be a long and tiring trip. Part of me says, "Why would I want to do this at 70? Shouldn't I just enjoy this phase of life?" I find myself comparing myself with others my age. But then I think of the last day, when Jesus will *not* say, "Let's talk about what

---

[72] We call our new ministry: *Life As It Ought to Be.*

others have done," but he may say, "Let's talk about that ministry opportunity in Tanzania…"

I want everything I do to be done in light of that day. I want to live *this day for that day.* That is *life as it ought to be.*

Conclusion

❧

Stand by the roads, and look, and ask for the ancient paths, where the good way is; and walk in it, and find rest for your souls.

Jeremiah 6:16

My friend David recently asked me, "So, what does a day of living *life as it ought to be* look like?" That made me think. Here is my best explanation of what it looks like for me to live *life as it ought to be.*

A day of living *life as it ought to be* is a day when I seek to live *in Christ, by the Spirit, to the glory of the Father.* I use those three phrases to remind myself how I am to live moment by moment.[73]

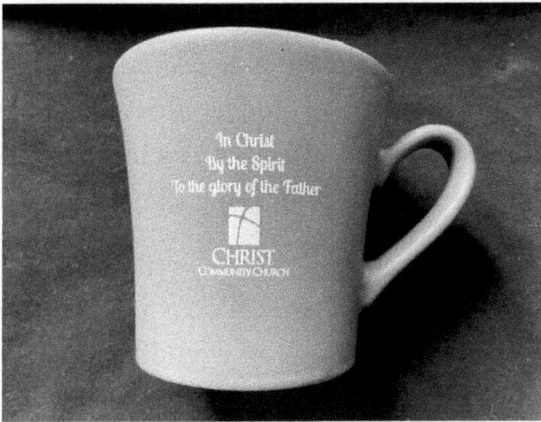

---

[73] At Christ Community Church, where I pastored, those phrases became so important to us that we put them on the mugs we gave out to guests. When I would drink my morning tea, my mug reminded me to live in Christ, by the Spirit, and to the glory of the Father.

155

A day of living *life as it ought to be* is a day when I intentionally seek to align my heart with the gospel as I begin and as I live out the day. For me, reading, pondering, praying, and then seeking to live and share God's words are essential parts of this life.

A day of living *life as it ought to be* is a day when I seek to live present tense, when I stop being in such a hurry, and when I cease focusing on what people think of me or how things might turn out. It is a day when I laugh with my wife. It is a day when I slow down enough to listen. It is a day when I live in the now.

Life as it ought to be is a day when I take time to slow down enough to enjoy the good things God has given. It is a day when I am aware of my union with Jesus, expect the power of the Spirit to be at work in me and through me, and pursue the glory of my great God. *Life as it ought to be* is when I go through my day with a joyful preoccupation with the God who made me.

A day of living *life as it ought to be* is a day when I intentionally take time to encourage and be encouraged by other Christians. It is a day when I speak the Word of God to others. It is a day when I stir up and am stirred up by my interactions with other believers. *Life as it ought to be* for me is becoming an agent of joy in a world that is too often joyless.

A day of living *life as it ought to be* is not perfection. It is not having everything go well. It is most often the opposite of that. It is a day when I stumble, a day when I am weak and insufficient. It is a day when I often need to repent and believe the gospel anew.

Life as it ought to be is not me looking good or accomplishing some great thing. It is me doing small things to the glory of a great God. It is God's power in my weakness.

A day of living *life as it ought to be* is a day when the cares of this world lose their power over the laughter of eternity. It is a day when the joy of eternity begins to invade the brokenness of the now. It is a day when I choose to live a defiant joy.

A day of living *life as it ought to be* is when I find a way to engage my world with the gospel. It is a day when I speak to someone else about Jesus. *Life as it ought to be* is a day when the excellencies of Jesus overflow in my words.

In summary, the essence of a day of living *life as it ought to be* is a day when I, moment by moment, live in gospel power, which is unleashed in day by day gospel practices that more and more produce in me the new joy, new love, and new boldness of spiritual awakening.

An Aisle Seat

Here is a story that illustrates the fruit of living life as it ought to be. I hasten to add that this kind of experience does not happen to me every day, and yet it wouldn't have happened if I had not begun to experience *life as it ought to be.*

In the fall of 2021, I flew from my new home in South Carolina to my home church of the last 35 years in north-central New Jersey to participate in the installation service for our church's new pastor. I bought the cheapest tickets, where they assign your seat at the last moment. I expected to get the most unwanted seat on the plane—the dreaded middle seat at the rear of the aircraft. As I waited, I pondered what it meant to live *in Christ, by the Spirit,* and *for the glory of the Father* for that day. I was thinking about what it meant for me to die to my agenda and plans so I could live the agenda of the Holy Spirit. Then, the flight attendant at the desk announced that the plane was full and they needed some passengers to be willing to check their carry-ons. I noticed that no one volunteered, probably because the point of having a carry-on is that you don't have the inconvenience of waiting for your bag. I thought, "I can do that."

So, I went to the desk, and the attendant thanked me and arranged for my carry-on to be checked. A short time later, they posted my seat: not a middle seat, but a coveted aisle seat! It was at the rear of the plane, but it was an aisle seat! With my long legs, an aisle seat makes the trip much more pleasant. It just feels less claustrophobic to me.

I took my place in my aisle seat and prepared to enjoy the flight. But minutes before take-off, a gentleman came to the back of the plane, and I overheard him ask the flight attendant if he could have an aisle seat. He was bigger than I was, so I understood why he wanted an aisle seat. The flight attendant said she would see what she could do, but it was just minutes until takeoff. She seemed stressed, and I suspected there were no aisle seats available.

Then, I did something uncharacteristic for me. I immediately stood up and said to the flight attendant, "He can have my seat." Usually, I would look around, hoping someone else would volunteer or that the problem would go away (without me giving up my aisle seat). The flight attendant looked relieved and thanked me; I had just solved her problem. So, that gentleman took my aisle seat. The flight attendant escorted me toward the front, and as we walked, she thanked me and commented, "I also noticed that you were the only one who volunteered to check your bag." What a reminder that people are watching us.

She then took me to a seat further forward, one between two women who had placed their belongings in the empty middle seat. As they were reluctantly removing their belongings from my new seat and as I was preparing to squeeze in between them, the flight attendant paused and said, "Oh, there is an empty seat across the aisle!" It was empty, and…it was an aisle seat. But it wasn't just an aisle seat but an aisle seat on an exit row. You usually pay more for exit row seats because there is more room. So, I sat down in my new roomy exit row aisle seat!

But that is not the end of the story. I sat down next to a young lady named Jill, and Jill and I spent almost two hours talking on the flight to Newark, New Jersey. We talked about all kinds of things, including what it means to know God through the gospel of Jesus. I told Jill that the gospel means good news. Jill had never been part of a church and did not understand the gospel, but she was a fast learner. Late in our discussion, as I talked about something related to the gospel, Jill suddenly volunteered, "Good news!"

Here is what I learned: I experience the Spirit's power as I am aware of my union with Jesus, expect the unexpected power of the Spirit, and pursue the Father's agenda. I experience *life as it ought to be* when I seek to intentionally walk the *gospel way.*

Process

Living the *gospel way* is a process. Reading a book like this will not produce an ongoing awakening. But if you intentionally, specifically, and daily seek to walk the *gospel way* described in this book, I believe that you will more and more experience the kind of ongoing awakening for which your heart yearns. And the truths of the gospel will form your soul. When my wife and I were in Bible college, one of our professors used the catchy phrase, "Repetition is theological mucilage!" Mucilage, for you younger folk, means glue. I like to rephrase it: "Repetition is gospel glue!" It is as we repeatedly, day after day and throughout our days, seek to live the gospel that Christ is formed in us, and more and more, we are awakened to the gospel.

If you would like more resources on living "life as it ought to be," please get in touch with Dennis at <u>denniscahill@pm.me</u>.

The Great Need

The great need of our day is not bigger buildings, more sophisticated strategies, or even better-preached theology. The great need of our day is for ordinary people to live in union with our extraordinary God. The great need is a return to the ancient paths of the gospel. "Stand by the roads, and look, and ask for the ancient paths, where the good way is; and walk in it, and find rest for your souls" (Jeremiah 6:16). The great need of our day is for the church of Jesus to be awakened to the wonder, glory, and power of the gospel lived out in faith.

The great need is for God's people to live the *gospel way*. That is *life as it ought to be.*

Appendix: The Sword of the Spirit Devotional Journey

~~~~~~

O ur hearts need to be renewed day by day (2 Corinthians 4:16). Psalm 105:4 tells us to "Seek the LORD and his strength; seek his presence continually!" The *Sword of the Spirit Devotional Journey* is a tool that helps us to seek renewal each day through Word and prayer. The name *Sword of the Spirit Devotional Journey* comes from Ephesians 6:17, where Paul tells us to take up "the sword of the Spirit, which is the word of God..." The *Sword of the Spirit Devotional Journey* is a focused time that enables us to live the gospel all the time.

What is the Sword of the Spirit Devotional Journey?

The *Sword of the Spirit Devotional Journey* (*the SOS Journey*) is not just a Bible reading plan but a *way* of reading the Bible. The *SOS Journey* teaches us to *read* the Bible carefully, to *ponder* the Bible deeply, to *pray* the Bible fervently, and then to go out and *live and share* the Bible faithfully. Here are the distinctives of this devotional adventure:

- The *Sword of the Spirit Devotional Journey* teaches us how to read the Bible. The essence of Bible study is observation, interpretation, and application. The *Journey* seeks to teach us to observe, interpret, and apply the Bible to our daily living.

- The *Sword of the Spirit Devotional Journey* is systematic. We read widely. The *SOS Journey* takes us through the Bible, from Genesis to Revelation.

- The *Sword of the Spirit Devotional Journey* is contemplative. We read narrowly, choosing a small portion of the day's readings to think about and ponder deeply. We need to take time to think deeply about the Word of God for it to take root in our hearts.

How Much Time Does the Sword of the Spirit Devotional Journey Take?

Our schedules will vary according to our life situations, but a good goal is to schedule a half hour each day, allowing time to read, ponder, and pray before we go out to live our day. Seek to schedule a particular time each day for the *SOS Journey*. We want to create a life habit that allows for flexibility. The most natural time for most will be the beginning of the day. A short saying that helps me is "Word before work."[74]

You may not have a half hour each day or be unable to complete the *SOS Journey* in a half hour. You can adjust the amount of reading you do to accommodate your schedule. Reading a portion of the Word of God, thinking deeply about it, and praying from it each day is vital.

Beginning the Sword of the Spirit Devotional Journey

To embark on the *SOS Journey,* you will need a Bible, a notebook or journal, a pen, and a plan for what to read (more on

---

[74] I adapted this saying from Dennis Henderson of the *6:4 Fellowship*, although he used "worship before work."

that in a moment). The Journey has four related aspects: we read, we ponder, we pray, and we live and share.

The tool of journaling helps us to read, ponder, pray, and live the Word of God.

Read

Start by writing the day's date on the top of a blank page in your notebook, then write the word "Read" or "Listen" with a box around it, and then, next to the box, the passage or passages you will read that day.

Read prayerfully

Before you begin reading, prepare your heart by confessing any known sin and asking God, as you read, to reveal his majesty and wonder "in the face of Jesus" (2 Corinthians 4:6). This step is critically important and often overlooked. We must be mindful that the Bible is not just a book, but the Word of God, and the Spirit uses it to speak to us. Consider praying the Lord's Prayer (Mathew 6:9-13) slowly and meditatively before you read. I often use an acronym I learned from John Piper: IOUSL.

I stand for incline. "Incline my heart to your testimonies..." (Ps. 119:36). **O** stands for open. "Open my eyes, that I may behold wondrous things out of your law" (Psalm 119:18). **U** stands for unite. "Teach me your way, O Lord, that I may walk in your truth; unite my heart to fear your name" (Ps. 86:11). **S** is for satisfy. "Satisfy us in the morning with your steadfast love" (Psalm 90:14). **L** stands for lead. "Lead me in your paths of love and righteousness" (Psalm 23:3).[75]

Read systematically

I recommend reading from both the Old and New Testaments each day. One way to do that is to use the *M'Cheyne Bible Calendar* as revised by D.A. Carson.[76] The *M'Cheyne Bible Calendar* lists four readings for each day in four columns. Carson's revised guide uses the first two readings for one year and the other two readings for the second year. You will read the Old Testament once and the New Testament and Psalms twice in two years.

An alternative plan is to begin with Genesis 1 (the beginning of the Old Testament) and Matthew 1 (the beginning of the New Testament). Each day, read one chapter from each Testament. This will take you through the Old Testament in about two and a half years and the New Testament in less than a year.

For some, reading two passages each day is too demanding. If that is so and you are using Carson's revision of the *M'Cheyne Bible Calendar*, limit your readings to the second reading for each day; that approach will take you through the New Testament and Psalms each year. Or, if you are using my alternative approach, read through one chapter of the New Testament each day.

---

[75] John Piper, *Reading the Bible Supernaturally* (Wheaton, IL: Crossway 2017), 255, 256, 272.

[76] http://www.edginet.org/mcheyne/year_carson_a4.pdf. You can use other Bible reading plans but I like *M'Cheyne's* because it takes you through the whole Bible and you read from the Old And New Testament each day.

Ponder

Next, write the word "Ponder" (or "think" or "consider" or "meditate") with a box around it. Prayerfully choose a smaller part of the day's reading to think about more deeply. Write the reference to this smaller portion next to the box with the word "ponder."

We want to think more deeply about this smaller portion of the day's reading. This is contemplation, reflection, or meditation. Deep contemplation helps us integrate the Word of God into all that we are.

Read this smaller passage slowly several times. Read it aloud if possible. As we think deeply about this smaller portion, three words will help us: observe, interpret, and apply.

Observe – What does it say?

The first step is to observe. Write out and underline the word "Observe" or simply the letter 'O'. Under "Observe," write out your observations from the passage. Here, you ask the question, "What does it say?" I often write out that question next to the word "observe." You observe what the author said to the people in his day and context. Just note what the passage says. It might seem simple and obvious, but observation is the key to understanding. Here, you are asking, "What did the author of the passage say to the original readers?" The focus here is on what the passage said to the specific people it was written to.

Interpret – What does it mean?

The second step is to seek to understand the meaning of the passage. Now you begin to interpret the passage (all literature needs to be interpreted — even this morning's newsfeed!). John Piper says meaning is "what the author intended to communicate by his words."[77] You write the word "Meaning" or the letter "M" on the left and underline it. Here, you ask the question, "What does it mean?" You are wrestling with the question, "What does the passage mean?" After observing what the author said, you need to wrestle with his intention and the divine intention.

Apply – What does it say to me today?

The last step is to apply the passage to ourselves. You can write and underline the word "Apply" or the letter "A." Observation is necessary to discern the meaning of the passage, and the meaning of the passage leads us to apply the passage. Now that you have taken some time to observe and seek to understand the meaning, you apply the truth and meaning of the passage to your life. The meaning of the passage must be personally experienced.[78] Application should be present tense and use first-person pronouns like 'I' or 'my.'

Why use a journal?

Journaling is one way we do what the Bible calls meditating. "This Book of the Law shall not depart from your mouth, but you shall meditate on it day and night, so that you may be careful to do according to all that is written in it. For then you will make your way prosperous, and then you will have good success" (Joshua 1:8).

In the New Testament, Jesus' mother, Mary, "treasured up all these things, pondering them in her heart" (Luke 2:19). She "stored up" in her heart the events of Jesus' early life. To meditate, then, is

---

[77] Piper, *Reading the Bible,* 301.
[78] Piper, *Reading the Bible,* 301.

to treasure or store up the truth of the gospel in our hearts. We meditate when we think deeply or ponder the truth of God. When we wrestle with what a verse says, means, and how it applies to our lives, we are meditating. God calls us to read and think deeply about what we read! We meditate when we ask questions like, "What do I do differently? How should I think differently? How am I to feel because of this passage? How do I speak differently? How will I live differently because of this passage?"

Sometimes, I spend most of my Bible study time on observation. On other days, I focus on meaning. But most often, I focus on the "apply" part of the thinking-through process. I wonder, imagine, and think about how the passage for that day should intersect with my life.

It's tempting to jump directly to "apply," but until we have rightly understood the meaning of the passage, we won't know how to apply Scripture correctly.

Pray

Now pray out of the passage. *We cannot fully live the passage until we have prayed the passage!* This is because Spirit-aided prayer (Ephesians 6:18) is how the gospel forms in our hearts. Write the word "Pray" in your journal with a box around it, and then pray through the passage. I often write out a short prayer next to the word "pray." Prayer is how we respond to God's Word, bringing our hearts into alignment with the truth of God.

When I pray the passage, I seek to *begin with God.* I seek to declare his worth out of the passage. What is there in this passage that causes you to worship God? Then, I seek to *surrender to God.* How do I submit my will to his will?

And then I *ask from God.* I pray first that the truth of this passage will shape my heart and life. But this is also the time to pray for specific needs—both my needs and the needs of others. I use the first pages of my journal to list ongoing prayer needs. On the first two pages, I list requests for my family, then I leave pages for requests for my ministry, for people I am praying for who need to believe in Jesus (what I call a "Gospel List"), and finally, I list miscellaneous prayer needs. I also leave a page for each day of the week. On Sundays, I pray for my pastors and our church service; on Mondays, I pray for missionaries, etc. You might do this differently.

Live and Share

The fourth element of the *Journey* is we "live and share." Here, we seek to *walk with God.* Write the words "Live and Share" with a box around it. Write out a single sentence or even a phrase that will help you live out the meaning of the portion you pondered for that day. Take a few moments to rest in that truth, and then go and live out the truth you have just been reading, thinking, and praying about. Throughout the day, as the Spirit reminds you of the reading and thinking you did earlier, reorient your life, heart, and thinking with God's truth. Pray without ceasing. This is how the Bible transforms us.

An essential part of living the truth of a passage of Scripture is sharing what you learned with someone else. We seek to live the truth of the passage and then look for opportunities to share it with others. Take the truth you wrote out under "live and share" and seek to share that truth with someone else during your day. This will help you and often will minister to others.

Here is an example of one of my journal entries:

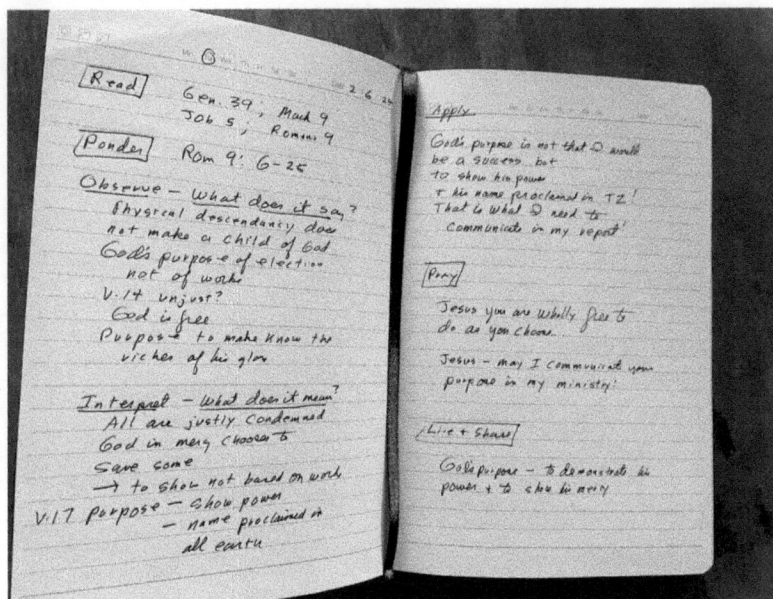

Family Devotions

For family devotions, read one chapter of the day's reading, or perhaps even part of a chapter, together as a family, and then talk about a verse or verses for a few minutes. Ask, "What does it mean?" and "How do we apply this passage?" And then pray together out of the passage. Begin with God in your praying. What is there to praise God for in the passage? Surrender to God. How do we respond to who God is? And ask from God. What do we need in the passage? Then, pray for other needs. Seek to have each family member participate—it should be a conversation, not a monologue.

www.ingramcontent.com/pod-product-compliance
Ingram Content Group UK Ltd.
Pitfield, Milton Keynes, MK11 3LW, UK
UKHW020713220925

8009UKWH00042B/653